TAJIK
VOCABULARY

ENGLISH-TAJIK

The most useful words
To expand your lexicon and sharpen
your language skills

3000 words

Tajik vocabulary for English speakers - 3000 words

By Andrey Taranov

T&P Books vocabularies are intended for helping you learn, memorize and review foreign words. The dictionary is divided into themes, covering all major spheres of everyday activities, business, science, culture, etc.

The process of learning words using T&P Books' theme-based dictionaries gives you the following advantages:

- Correctly grouped source information predetermines success at subsequent stages of word memorization
- Availability of words derived from the same root allowing memorization of word units (rather than separate words)
- Small units of words facilitate the process of establishing associative links needed for consolidation of vocabulary
- Level of language knowledge can be estimated by the number of learned words

T&P Books Publishing
www.tpbooks.com

ISBN: 978-1-78400-230-5

This book is also available in E-book formats.
Please visit www.tpbooks.com or the major online bookstores.

TAJIK VOCABULARY
for English speakers

T&P Books vocabularies are intended to help you learn, memorize, and review foreign words. The vocabulary contains over 3000 commonly used words arranged thematically.

* Vocabulary contains the most commonly used words
* Recommended as an addition to any language course
* Meets the needs of beginners and advanced learners of foreign languages
* Convenient for daily use, revision sessions, and self-testing activities
* Allows you to assess your vocabulary

Special features of the vocabulary

* Words are organized according to their meaning, not alphabetically
* Words are presented in three columns to facilitate the reviewing and self-testing processes
* Words in groups are divided into small blocks to facilitate the learning process
* The vocabulary offers a convenient and simple transcription of each foreign word

The vocabulary has 101 topics including:

Basic Concepts, Numbers, Colors, Months, Seasons, Units of Measurement, Clothing & Accessories, Food & Nutrition, Restaurant, Family Members, Relatives, Character, Feelings, Emotions, Diseases, City, Town, Sightseeing, Shopping, Money, House, Home, Office, Working in the Office, Import & Export, Marketing, Job Search, Sports, Education, Computer, Internet, Tools, Nature, Countries, Nationalities and more ...

T&P BOOKS' THEME-BASED DICTIONARIES

The Correct System for Memorizing Foreign Words

Acquiring vocabulary is one of the most important elements of learning a foreign language, because words allow us to express our thoughts, ask questions, and provide answers. An inadequate vocabulary can impede communication with a foreigner and make it difficult to understand a book or movie well.

The pace of activity in all spheres of modern life, including the learning of modern languages, has increased. Today, we need to memorize large amounts of information (grammar rules, foreign words, etc.) within a short period. However, this does not need to be difficult. All you need to do is to choose the right training materials, learn a few special techniques, and develop your individual training system.

Having a system is critical to the process of language learning. Many people fail to succeed in this regard; they cannot master a foreign language because they fail to follow a system comprised of selecting materials, organizing lessons, arranging new words to be learned, and so on. The lack of a system causes confusion and eventually, lowers self-confidence.

T&P Books' theme-based dictionaries can be included in the list of elements needed for creating an effective system for learning foreign words. These dictionaries were specially developed for learning purposes and are meant to help students effectively memorize words and expand their vocabulary.

Generally speaking, the process of learning words consists of three main elements:

- Reception (creation or acquisition) of a training material, such as a word list
- Work aimed at memorizing new words
- Work aimed at reviewing the learned words, such as self-testing

All three elements are equally important since they determine the quality of work and the final result. All three processes require certain skills and a well-thought-out approach.

New words are often encountered quite randomly when learning a foreign language and it may be difficult to include them all in a unified list. As a result, these words remain written on scraps of paper, in book margins, textbooks, and so on. In order to systematize such words, we have to create and continually update a "book of new words." A paper notebook, a netbook, or a tablet PC can be used for these purposes.

This "book of new words" will be your personal, unique list of words. However, it will only contain the words that you came across during the learning process. For example, you might have written down the words "Sunday," "Tuesday," and "Friday." However, there are additional words for days of the week, for example, "Saturday," that are missing, and your list of words would be incomplete. Using a theme dictionary, in addition to the "book of new words," is a reasonable solution to this problem.

The theme-based dictionary may serve as the basis for expanding your vocabulary.

It will be your big "book of new words" containing the most frequently used words of a foreign language already included. There are quite a few theme-based dictionaries available, and you should ensure that you make the right choice in order to get the maximum benefit from your purchase.

Therefore, we suggest using theme-based dictionaries from T&P Books Publishing as an aid to learning foreign words. Our books are specially developed for effective use in the sphere of vocabulary systematization, expansion and review.

Theme-based dictionaries are not a magical solution to learning new words. However, they can serve as your main database to aid foreign-language acquisition. Apart from theme dictionaries, you can have copybooks for writing down new words, flash cards, glossaries for various texts, as well as other resources; however, a good theme dictionary will always remain your primary collection of words.

T&P Books' theme-based dictionaries are specialty books that contain the most frequently used words in a language.

The main characteristic of such dictionaries is the division of words into themes. For example, the *City* theme contains the words "street," "crossroads," "square," "fountain," and so on. The *Talking* theme might contain words like "to talk," "to ask," "question," and "answer".

All the words in a theme are divided into smaller units, each comprising 3–5 words. Such an arrangement improves the perception of words and makes the learning process less tiresome. Each unit contains a selection of words with similar meanings or identical roots. This allows you to learn words in small groups and establish other associative links that have a positive effect on memorization.

The words on each page are placed in three columns: a word in your native language, its translation, and its transcription. Such positioning allows for the use of techniques for effective memorization. After closing the translation column, you can flip through and review foreign words, and vice versa. "This is an easy and convenient method of review – one that we recommend you do often."

Our theme-based dictionaries contain transcriptions for all the foreign words. Unfortunately, none of the existing transcriptions are able to convey the exact nuances of foreign pronunciation. That is why we recommend using the transcriptions only as a supplementary learning aid. Correct pronunciation can only be acquired with the help of sound. Therefore our collection includes audio theme-based dictionaries.

The process of learning words using T&P Books' theme-based dictionaries gives you the following advantages:

- You have correctly grouped source information, which predetermines your success at subsequent stages of word memorization
- Availability of words derived from the same root (lazy, lazily, lazybones), allowing you to memorize word units instead of separate words
- Small units of words facilitate the process of establishing associative links needed for consolidation of vocabulary
- You can estimate the number of learned words and hence your level of language knowledge
- The dictionary allows for the creation of an effective and high-quality revision process
- You can revise certain themes several times, modifying the revision methods and techniques
- Audio versions of the dictionaries help you to work out the pronunciation of words and develop your skills of auditory word perception

The T&P Books' theme-based dictionaries are offered in several variants differing in the number of words: 1.500, 3.000, 5.000, 7.000, and 9.000 words. There are also dictionaries containing 15,000 words for some language combinations. Your choice of dictionary will depend on your knowledge level and goals.

We sincerely believe that our dictionaries will become your trusty assistant in learning foreign languages and will allow you to easily acquire the necessary vocabulary.

TABLE OF CONTENTS

PRONUNCIATION GUIDE

Letter	Tajik example	T&P phonetic alphabet	English example
А а	Раҳмат!	[a]	shorter than in ask
Б б	бесоҳиб	[b]	baby, book
В в	вафодорй	[v]	very, river
Г г	гулмохӣ	[g]	game, gold
Ғ ғ	мурғобӣ	[ʁ]	French (guttural) R
Д д	мадд	[d]	day, doctor
Е е	телескоп	[e:]	longer than in bell
Ё ё	сайёра	[jɔ]	New York
Ж ж	аждаҳо	[ʒ]	forge, pleasure
З з	сӯзанда	[z]	zebra, please
И и	шифт	[i]	shorter than in feet
Й й	обчакорӣ	[i:]	feet, meter
Й й	ҳайкал	[j]	yes, New York
К к	коргардон	[k]	clock, kiss
Қ қ	нуқта	[q]	king, club
Л л	пилла	[l]	lace, people
М м	мусиқачӣ	[m]	magic, milk
Н н	нонвой	[n]	sang, thing
О о	посбон	[o:]	fall, bomb
П п	папка	[p]	pencil, private
Р р	чароғак	[r]	rice, radio
С с	суръат	[s]	city, boss
Т т	тарқиш	[t]	tourist, trip
У у	муҳаррик	[u]	book
Ӯ ӯ	кӯшк	[œ]	German Hölle
Ф ф	фурӯш	[f]	face, food
Х х	хушксолӣ	[x]	as in Scots 'loch'
Ҳ ҳ	чарогоҳ	[h]	home, have
Ч ч	чароғ	[ʧ]	church, French
Ҷ ҷ	ҷанҷол	[ʤ]	joke, general
Ш ш	нашриёт	[ʃ]	machine, shark
Ъ ъ [1]	таърихдон	[:], [ˈ]	no sound
Э э	эҳтимолӣ	[ɛ]	man, bad
Ю ю	юнонӣ	[ju]	youth, usually
Я я	яхбурча	[ja]	Kenya, piano

Comments

[1] [:] - Lengthens the preceding vowel; ['] - after consonants is used as a 'hard sign'

ABBREVIATIONS
used in the vocabulary

English abbreviations

ab.	-	about
adj	-	adjective
adv	-	adverb
anim.	-	animate
as adj	-	attributive noun used as adjective
e.g.	-	for example
etc.	-	et cetera
fam.	-	familiar
fem.	-	feminine
form.	-	formal
inanim.	-	inanimate
masc.	-	masculine
math	-	mathematics
mil.	-	military
n	-	noun
pl	-	plural
pron.	-	pronoun
sb	-	somebody
sing.	-	singular
sth	-	something
v aux	-	auxiliary verb
vi	-	intransitive verb
vi, vt	-	intransitive, transitive verb
vt	-	transitive verb

BASIC CONCEPTS

1. Pronouns

I, me	ман	[man]
you	ту	[tu]
he	ӯ, вай	[œ], [vaj]
she	ӯ, вай	[œ], [vaj]
it	он	[on]
we	мо	[mo]
you (to a group)	шумо	[ʃumo]
you (polite, sing.)	Шумо	[ʃumo]
you (polite, pl)	Шумо	[ʃumo]
they (inanim.)	онон	[onon]
they (anim.)	онҳо, вайҳо	[onho], [vajho]

2. Greetings. Salutations

Hello! (fam.)	Салом!	[salom]
Hello! (form.)	Ассалом!	[assalom]
Good morning!	Субҳатон ба хайр!	[subhaton ba χajr]
Good afternoon!	Рӯз ба хайр!	[rœz ba χajr]
Good evening!	Шом ба хайр!	[ʃom ba χajr]
to say hello	саломалейк кардан	[salomalejk kardan]
Hi! (hello)	Ассалом! Салом!	[assalom salom]
greeting (n)	вохӯрдӣ	[voχœrdi:]
to greet (vt)	вохӯрдӣ кардан	[voχœrdi: kardan]
How are you? (form.)	Корҳоятон чӣ хел?	[korhojaton tʃi: χel]
How are you? (fam.)	Корҳоят чӣ хел?	[korhojat tʃi: χel]
What's new?	Чӣ навигарӣ?	[tʃi: navigari:]
Goodbye! (form.)	То дидан!	[to didan]
Bye! (fam.)	Хайр!	[χajr]
See you soon!	То вохӯрии наздик!	[to voχœri:i nazdik]
Farewell! (to a friend)	Падруд!	[padrud]
Farewell! (form.)	Хайрбод! Падруд!	[χajrbod padrud]
to say goodbye	падруд гуфтан	[padrud guftan]
So long!	Хайр!	[χajr]
Thank you!	Раҳмат!	[rahmat]
Thank you very much!	Бисёр раҳмат!	[bisjor rahmat]

You're welcome	Марҳамат!	[marhamat]
Don't mention it!	Намеарзад	[namearzad]
It was nothing	Намеарзад	[namearzad]

Excuse me! (fam.)	Бубахш!	[bubaχʃ]
Excuse me! (form.)	Бубахшед!	[bubaχʃed]
to excuse (forgive)	афв кардан	[afv kardan]

to apologize (vi)	узр пурсидан	[uzr pursidan]
My apologies	Маро бубахшед	[maro bubaχʃed]
I'm sorry!	Бубахшед!	[bubaχʃed]
to forgive (vt)	бахшидан	[baχʃidan]
It's okay! (that's all right)	Ҳеч гап не	[hetʃ gap ne]
please (adv)	илтимос	[iltimos]

Don't forget!	Фаромӯш накунед!	[faromœʃ nakuned]
Certainly!	Албатта!	[albatta]
Of course not!	Албатта не!	[albatta ne]
Okay! (I agree)	Розӣ!	[rozi:]
That's enough!	Бас!	[bas]

3. Questions

Who?	Кӣ?	[ki:]
What?	Чӣ?	[tʃi:]
Where? (at, in)	Дар куҷо?	[dar kudʒo]
Where (to)?	Куҷо?	[kudʒo]
From where?	Аз куҷо?	[az kudʒo]
When?	Кай?	[kaj]
Why? (What for?)	Барои чӣ?	[baroi tʃi:]
Why? (~ are you crying?)	Барои чӣ?	[baroi tʃi:]

What for?	Барои чӣ?	[baroi tʃi:]
How? (in what way)	Чӣ хел?	[tʃi: χel]
What? (What kind of ...?)	Кадом?	[kadom]
Which?	Чанд? Чандум?	[tʃand tʃandum]
To whom?	Ба кӣ?	[ba ki:]
About whom?	Дар бораи кӣ?	[dar borai ki:]
About what?	Дар бораи чӣ?	[dar borai tʃi:]
With whom?	Бо кӣ?	[bo ki:]
How many?	Чанд-то?	[tʃand-to]
How much?	Чӣ қадар?	[tʃi: qadar]
Whose?	Аз они кӣ?	[az oni ki:]

4. Prepositions

| with (accompanied by) | бо, ҳамроҳи | [bo], [hamrohi] |
| without | бе | [be] |

to (indicating direction)	ба	[ba]
about (talking ~ ...)	дар бораи	[dar borai]
before (in time)	пеш аз	[peʃ az]
in front of ...	дар пеши	[dar peʃi]

under (beneath, below)	таги	[tagi]
above (over)	дар болои	[dar boloi]
on (atop)	ба болои	[ba boloi]
from (off, out of)	аз	[az]
of (made from)	аз	[az]

| in (e.g., ~ ten minutes) | баъд аз | [ba'd az] |
| over (across the top of) | аз болои ... | [az boloi] |

5. Function words. Adverbs. Part 1

Where? (at, in)	Дар куҷо?	[dar kudʒo]
here (adv)	ин ҷо	[in dʒo]
there (adv)	он ҷо	[on dʒo]

| somewhere (to be) | дар куҷое | [dar kudʒoe] |
| nowhere (not anywhere) | дар ҳеҷ ҷо | [dar hedʒ dʒo] |

| by (near, beside) | дар назди ... | [dar nazdi] |
| by the window | дар назди тиреза | [dar nazdi tireza] |

Where (to)?	Куҷо?	[kudʒo]
here (e.g., come ~!)	ин ҷо	[in tʃo]
there (e.g., to go ~)	ба он ҷо	[ba on dʒo]
from here (adv)	аз ин ҷо	[az in dʒo]
from there (adv)	аз он ҷо	[az on dʒo]

| close (adv) | наздик | [nazdik] |
| far (adv) | дур | [dur] |

near (e.g., ~ Paris)	дар бари	[dar bari]
nearby (adv)	бисёр наздик	[bisjor nazdik]
not far (adv)	наздик	[nazdik]

left (adj)	чап	[tʃap]
on the left	аз чап	[az tʃap]
to the left	ба тарафи чап	[ba tarafi tʃap]

right (adj)	рост	[rost]
on the right	аз рост	[az rost]
to the right	ба тарафи рост	[ba tarafi rost]

in front (adv)	аз пеш	[az peʃ]
front (as adj)	пешин	[peʃin]
ahead (the kids ran ~)	ба пеш	[ba peʃ]

behind (adv)	дар қафои	[dar qafoi]
from behind	аз қафо	[az qafo]
back (towards the rear)	ақиб	[aqib]

| middle | миёна | [mijɔna] |
| in the middle | дар миёна | [dar mijɔna] |

at the side	аз паҳлу	[az pahlu]
everywhere (adv)	дар ҳар ҷо	[dar har ʤo]
around (in all directions)	гирду атроф	[girdu atrof]

from inside	аз дарун	[az darun]
somewhere (to go)	ба ким-кучо	[ba kim-kuʤo]
straight (directly)	миёнбур карда	[mijɔnbur karda]
back (e.g., come ~)	ба ақиб	[ba aqib]

| from anywhere | аз ягон ҷо | [az jagon ʤo] |
| from somewhere | аз як ҷо | [az jak ʤo] |

firstly (adv)	аввалан	[avvalan]
secondly (adv)	дуюм	[dujum]
thirdly (adv)	сеюм	[sejum]

suddenly (adv)	ногоҳ, баногоҳ	[nogoh], [banogoh]
at first (in the beginning)	дар аввал	[dar avval]
for the first time	якумин	[jakumin]
long before …	хеле пеш	[χele peʃ]
anew (over again)	аз нав	[az nav]
for good (adv)	тамоман	[tamoman]

never (adv)	ҳеҷ гоҳ	[heʤ goh]
again (adv)	боз, аз дигар	[boz], [az digar]
now (adv)	акнун	[aknun]
often (adv)	тез-тез	[tez-tez]
then (adv)	он вақт	[on vaqt]
urgently (quickly)	зуд, фавран	[zud], [favran]
usually (adv)	одатан	[odatan]

by the way, …	воқеан	[voqean]
possible (that is ~)	шояд	[ʃojad]
probably (adv)	эҳтимол	[ɛhtimol]
maybe (adv)	эҳтимол, шояд	[ɛhtimol], [ʃojad]
besides …	ғайр аз он	[ʁajr az on]
that's why …	бинобар ин	[binobar in]
in spite of …	ба ин нигоҳ накарда	[ba in nigoh nakarda]
thanks to …	ба туфайли …	[ba tufajli]

what (pron.)	чӣ	[ʧi:]
that (conj.)	ки	[ki]
something	чизе	[ʧize]
anything (something)	ягон чиз	[jagon ʧiz]
nothing	ҳеҷ чиз	[heʤ ʧiz]

who (pron.)	кӣ	[kiː]
someone	ким-кӣ	[kim-kiː]
somebody	касе	[kase]

nobody	ҳеҷ кас	[hedʒ kas]
nowhere (a voyage to ~)	ба ҳеҷ куҷо	[ba hedʒ kudʒo]
nobody's	бесоҳиб	[besohib]
somebody's	аз они касе	[az oni kase]

so (I'm ~ glad)	чунон	[tʃunon]
also (as well)	ҳам	[ham]
too (as well)	низ, ҳам	[niz], [ham]

6. Function words. Adverbs. Part 2

Why?	Барои чӣ?	[baroi tʃiː]
for some reason	бо ким-кадом сабаб	[bo kim-kadom sabab]
because ...	зеро ки	[zero ki]
for some purpose	барои чизе	[baroi tʃize]

and	ва, ... у, ... ю	[va], [u], [ju]
or	ё	[jɔ]
but	аммо, лекин	[ammo], [lekin]
for (e.g., ~ me)	барои	[baroi]

too (~ many people)	аз меъёр зиёд	[az me'jɔr zijɔd]
only (exclusively)	фақат	[faqat]
exactly (adv)	айнан	[ajnan]
about (more or less)	тақрибан	[taqriban]

approximately (adv)	тақрибан	[taqriban]
approximate (adj)	тақрибӣ	[taqribiː]
almost (adv)	қариб	[qarib]
the rest	боқимонда	[bɔqimonda]

the other (second)	дигар	[digar]
other (different)	дигар	[digar]
each (adj)	ҳар	[har]
any (no matter which)	ҳар	[har]
many, much (a lot of)	бисёр, хеле	[bisjɔr], [χele]
many people	бисёриҳо	[bisjɔriho]
all (everyone)	ҳама	[hama]

in return for ...	ба ивази	[ba ivazi]
in exchange (adv)	ба ивазаш	[ba ivazaʃ]
by hand (made)	дастӣ	[dastiː]
hardly (negative opinion)	ба гумон	[ba gumon]

| probably (adv) | эҳтимол, шояд | [ɛhtimol], [ʃojad] |
| on purpose (intentionally) | барқасд | [barqasd] |

by accident (adv)	тасодуфан	[tasodufan]
very (adv)	хеле	[χele]
for example (adv)	масалан, чунончи	[masalan], [tʃunontʃi]
between	дар байни	[dar bajni]
among	дар байни ...	[dar bajni]
so much (such a lot)	ин қадар	[in qadar]
especially (adv)	хусусан	[χususan]

NUMBERS. MISCELLANEOUS

7. Cardinal numbers. Part 1

0 zero	сифр	[sifr]
1 one	як	[jak]
2 two	ду	[du]
3 three	се	[se]
4 four	чор, чахор	[tʃor], [tʃahor]
5 five	панч	[pandʒ]
6 six	шаш	[ʃaʃ]
7 seven	хафт	[haft]
8 eight	хашт	[haʃt]
9 nine	нух	[nuh]
10 ten	дах	[dah]
11 eleven	ёздах	[jozdah]
12 twelve	дувоздах	[duvozdah]
13 thirteen	сездах	[sezdah]
14 fourteen	чордах	[tʃordah]
15 fifteen	понздах	[ponzdah]
16 sixteen	шонздах	[ʃonzdah]
17 seventeen	хафдах	[hafdah]
18 eighteen	хаждах	[haʒdah]
19 nineteen	нуздах	[nuzdah]
20 twenty	бист	[bist]
21 twenty-one	бисту як	[bistu jak]
22 twenty-two	бисту ду	[bistu du]
23 twenty-three	бисту се	[bistu se]
30 thirty	сй	[si:]
31 thirty-one	сию як	[siju jak]
32 thirty-two	сию ду	[siju du]
33 thirty-three	сию се	[siju se]
40 forty	чил	[tʃil]
41 forty-one	чилу як	[tʃilu jak]
42 forty-two	чилу ду	[tʃilu du]
43 forty-three	чилу се	[tʃilu se]
50 fifty	панчох	[pandʒoh]
51 fifty-one	панчоху як	[pandʒohu jak]
52 fifty-two	панчоху ду	[pandʒohu du]

53 fifty-three	панҷоҳу се	[pandʒohu se]
60 sixty	шаст	[ʃast]
61 sixty-one	шасту як	[ʃastu jak]
62 sixty-two	шасту ду	[ʃastu du]
63 sixty-three	шасту се	[ʃastu se]
70 seventy	ҳафтод	[haftod]
71 seventy-one	ҳафтоду як	[haftodu jak]
72 seventy-two	ҳафтоду ду	[haftodu du]
73 seventy-three	ҳафтоду се	[haftodu se]
80 eighty	ҳаштод	[haʃtod]
81 eighty-one	ҳаштоду як	[haʃtodu jak]
82 eighty-two	ҳаштоду ду	[haʃtodu du]
83 eighty-three	ҳаштоду се	[haʃtodu se]
90 ninety	навад	[navad]
91 ninety-one	наваду як	[navadu jak]
92 ninety-two	наваду ду	[navadu du]
93 ninety-three	наваду се	[navadu se]

8. Cardinal numbers. Part 2

100 one hundred	сад	[sad]
200 two hundred	дусад	[dusad]
300 three hundred	сесад	[sesad]
400 four hundred	чорсад, чаҳорсад	[tʃorsad], [tʃahorsad]
500 five hundred	панҷсад	[pandʒsad]
600 six hundred	шашсад	[ʃaʃsad]
700 seven hundred	ҳафтсад	[haftsad]
800 eight hundred	ҳаштсад	[haʃtsad]
900 nine hundred	нӯҳсадум	[nœhsadum]
1000 one thousand	ҳазор	[hazor]
2000 two thousand	ду ҳазор	[du hazor]
3000 three thousand	се ҳазор	[se hazor]
10000 ten thousand	даҳ ҳазор	[dah hazor]
one hundred thousand	сад ҳазор	[sad hazor]
million	миллион	[million]
billion	миллиард	[milliard]

9. Ordinal numbers

first (adj)	якум	[jakum]
second (adj)	дуюм	[dujum]
third (adj)	сеюм	[sejum]
fourth (adj)	чорум	[tʃorum]

fifth (adj)	панҷум	[pandʒum]
sixth (adj)	шашум	[ʃaʃum]
seventh (adj)	ҳафтум	[haftum]
eighth (adj)	ҳаштум	[haʃtum]
ninth (adj)	нӯхум	[nœhum]
tenth (adj)	даҳӯм	[dahœm]

COLOURS. UNITS OF MEASUREMENT

10. Colors

color	ранг	[rang]
shade (tint)	тобиш	[tobiʃ]
hue	тобиш, лавн	[tobiʃ], [lavn]
rainbow	рангинкамон	[ranginkamon]
white (adj)	сафед	[safed]
black (adj)	сиёҳ	[sijoh]
gray (adj)	адкан	[adkan]
green (adj)	сабз, кабуд	[sabz], [kabud]
yellow (adj)	зард	[zard]
red (adj)	сурх, арғувонӣ	[surχ], [arʁuvoni:]
blue (adj)	кабуд	[kabud]
light blue (adj)	осмонӣ	[osmoni:]
pink (adj)	гулобӣ	[gulobi:]
orange (adj)	норанчӣ	[norandʒi:]
violet (adj)	бунафш	[bunafʃ]
brown (adj)	қаҳвагӣ	[qahvagi:]
golden (adj)	тиллоранг	[tillorang]
silvery (adj)	нуқрафом	[nuqrafom]
beige (adj)	каҳваранг	[kahvarang]
cream (adj)	зардтоб	[zardtob]
turquoise (adj)	фирӯзаранг	[firœzarang]
cherry red (adj)	олуболугӣ	[olubolugi:]
lilac (adj)	бунафш, нофармон	[bunafʃ], [nofarmon]
crimson (adj)	сурхи сиеҳтоб	[surχi siehtob]
light (adj)	кушод	[kuʃod]
dark (adj)	торик	[torik]
bright, vivid (adj)	тоза	[toza]
colored (pencils)	ранга	[ranga]
color (e.g., ~ film)	ранга	[ranga]
black-and-white (adj)	сиёҳу сафед	[sijohu safed]
plain (one-colored)	якранга	[jakranga]
multicolored (adj)	рангоранг	[rangorang]

11. Units of measurement

weight	вазн	[vazn]
length	дарозӣ	[darozi:]
width	арз	[arz]
height	баландӣ	[balandi:]
depth	чуқурӣ	[tʃuquri:]
volume	ҳаҷм	[hadʒm]
area	масоҳат	[masohat]
gram	грам	[gram]
milligram	миллиграмм	[milligramm]
kilogram	килограмм	[kilogramm]
ton	тонна	[tonna]
pound	қадоқ	[qadoq]
ounce	вақия	[vaqija]
meter	метр	[metr]
millimeter	миллиметр	[millimetr]
centimeter	сантиметр	[santimetr]
kilometer	километр	[kilometr]
mile	мил	[mil]
foot	фут	[fut]
yard	ярд	[jard]
square meter	метри квадратӣ	[metri kvadrati:]
hectare	гектар	[gektar]
liter	литр	[litr]
degree	дараҷа	[daradʒa]
volt	волт	[volt]
ampere	ампер	[amper]
horsepower	қувваи асп	[quvvai asp]
quantity	миқдор	[miqdor]
a little bit of …	камтар	[kamtar]
half	нисф	[nisf]
piece (item)	дона	[dona]
size	ҳаҷм	[hadʒm]
scale (map ~)	масштаб	[masʃtab]
minimal (adj)	камтарин	[kamtarin]
the smallest (adj)	хурдтарин	[xurdtarin]
medium (adj)	миёна	[mijɔna]
maximal (adj)	ниҳоят калон	[nihojat kalon]
the largest (adj)	калонтарин	[kalontarin]

12. Containers

canning jar (glass ~)	банкаи шишагӣ	[bankai ʃiʃagi:]
can	банкаи тунукагӣ	[bankai tunukagi:]
bucket	сатил	[satil]
barrel	бочка, чалак	[botʃka], [tʃalak]
wash basin (e.g., plastic ~)	тағора	[taʁora]
tank (100L water ~)	бак, чалак	[bak], [tʃalak]
hip flask	обдон	[obdon]
jerrycan	канистра	[kanistra]
tank (e.g., tank car)	систерна	[sisterna]
mug	кружка, дӯлча	[kruʒka], [dœltʃa]
cup (of coffee, etc.)	косача	[kosatʃa]
saucer	тақсимӣ, тақсимича	[taqsimi:], [taqsimitʃa]
glass (tumbler)	стакан	[stakan]
wine glass	бокал	[bokal]
stock pot (soup pot)	дегча	[degtʃa]
bottle (~ of wine)	шиша, сурохӣ	[ʃiʃa], [surohi:]
neck (of the bottle, etc.)	даҳани шиша	[dahani ʃiʃa]
carafe (decanter)	сурохӣ	[surohi:]
pitcher	кӯза	[kœza]
vessel (container)	зарф	[zarf]
pot (crock, stoneware ~)	хурмача	[xurmatʃa]
vase	гулдон	[guldon]
bottle (perfume ~)	шиша	[ʃiʃa]
vial, small bottle	хубобча	[hubobtʃa]
tube (of toothpaste)	лӯлача	[lœlatʃa]
sack (bag)	халта	[xalta]
bag (paper ~, plastic ~)	халта	[xalta]
pack (of cigarettes, etc.)	қуттӣ	[qutti:]
box (e.g., shoebox)	қуттӣ	[qutti:]
crate	қуттӣ	[qutti:]
basket	сабад	[sabad]

MAIN VERBS

13. The most important verbs. Part 1

to advise (vt)	маслиҳат додан	[maslihat dodan]
to agree (say yes)	розигӣ додан	[rozigi: dodan]
to answer (vi, vt)	ҷавоб додан	[dʒavob dodan]
to apologize (vi)	узр пурсидан	[uzr pursidan]
to arrive (vi)	расидан	[rasidan]
to ask (~ oneself)	пурсидан	[pursidan]
to ask (~ sb to do sth)	пурсидан	[pursidan]
to be (vi)	будан	[budan]
to be afraid	тарсидан	[tarsidan]
to be hungry	хӯрок хостан	[xœrok xostan]
to be interested in …	ҳавас кардан	[havas kardan]
to be needed	даркор будан	[darkor budan]
to be surprised	ба ҳайрат афтодан	[ba hajrat aftodan]
to be thirsty	об хостан	[ob xostan]
to begin (vt)	сар кардан	[sar kardan]
to belong to …	таалуқ доштан	[taaluq doʃtan]
to boast (vi)	худситой кардан	[xudsitoi: kardan]
to break (split into pieces)	шикастан	[ʃikastan]
to call (~ for help)	чеғ задан	[dʒeʁ zadan]
can (v aux)	тавонистан	[tavonistan]
to catch (vt)	доштан	[doʃtan]
to change (vt)	иваз кардан	[ivaz kardan]
to choose (select)	интихоб кардан	[intixob kardan]
to come down (the stairs)	фуромадан	[furomadan]
to compare (vt)	муқоиса кардан	[muqoisa kardan]
to complain (vi, vt)	шикоят кардан	[ʃikojat kardan]
to confuse (mix up)	иштибоҳ кардан	[iʃtiboh kardan]
to continue (vt)	давомат кардан	[davomat kardan]
to control (vt)	назорат кардан	[nazorat kardan]
to cook (dinner)	пухтан	[puxtan]
to cost (vt)	арзидан	[arzidan]
to count (add up)	ҳисоб кардан	[hisob kardan]
to count on …	умед бастан	[umed bastan]
to create (vt)	офаридан	[ofaridan]
to cry (weep)	гиря кардан	[girja kardan]

14. The most important verbs. Part 2

to deceive (vi, vt)	фирефтан	[fireftan]
to decorate (tree, street)	оростан	[orostan]
to defend (a country, etc.)	муҳофиза кардан	[muhofiza kardan]
to demand (request firmly)	талаб кардан	[talab kardan]
to dig (vt)	кофтан	[koftan]
to discuss (vt)	муҳокима кардан	[muhokima kardan]
to do (vt)	кардан	[kardan]
to doubt (have doubts)	шак доштан	[ʃak doʃtan]
to drop (let fall)	афтондан	[aftondan]
to enter (room, house, etc.)	даромадан	[daromadan]
to excuse (forgive)	афв кардан	[afv kardan]
to exist (vi)	зиндагӣ кардан	[zindagi: kardan]
to expect (foresee)	пешбинӣ кардан	[peʃbini: kardan]
to explain (vt)	шарҳ додан	[ʃarh dodan]
to fall (vi)	афтодан	[aftodan]
to find (vt)	ёфтан	[joftan]
to finish (vt)	тамом кардан	[tamom kardan]
to fly (vi)	паридан	[paridan]
to follow ... (come after)	рафтан	[raftan]
to forget (vi, vt)	фаромӯш кардан	[faromœʃ kardan]
to forgive (vt)	бахшидан	[baxʃidan]
to give (vt)	додан	[dodan]
to give a hint	луқма додан	[luqma dodan]
to go (on foot)	рафтан	[raftan]
to go for a swim	оббозӣ кардан	[obbozi: kardan]
to go out (for dinner, etc.)	баромадан	[baromadan]
to guess (the answer)	ёфтан	[joftan]
to have (vt)	доштан	[doʃtan]
to have breakfast	ноништа кардан	[noniʃta kardan]
to have dinner	хӯроки шом хӯрдан	[xœroki ʃom xœrdan]
to have lunch	хӯроки пешин хӯрдан	[xœroki peʃin xœrdan]
to hear (vt)	шунидан	[ʃunidan]
to help (vt)	кумак кардан	[kumak kardan]
to hide (vt)	пинҳон кардан	[pinhon kardan]
to hope (vi, vt)	умед доштан	[umed doʃtan]
to hunt (vi, vt)	шикор кардан	[ʃikor kardan]
to hurry (vi)	шитоб кардан	[ʃitob kardan]

15. The most important verbs. Part 3

to inform (vt)	ахборот додан	[aχborot dodan]
to insist (vi, vt)	сахт истодан	[saχt istodan]
to insult (vt)	таҳқир кардан	[tahqir kardan]
to invite (vt)	даъват кардан	[da'vat kardan]
to joke (vi)	шӯхӣ кардан	[ʃœχi: kardan]
to keep (vt)	нигоҳ доштан	[nigoh doʃtan]
to keep silent	хомӯш будан	[χomœʃ budan]
to kill (vt)	куштан	[kuʃtan]
to know (sb)	донистан	[donistan]
to know (sth)	донистан	[donistan]
to laugh (vi)	хандидан	[χandidan]
to liberate (city, etc.)	озод кардан	[ozod kardan]
to like (I like …)	форидан	[foridan]
to look for … (search)	ҷустан	[dʒustan]
to love (sb)	дӯст доштан	[dœst doʃtan]
to make a mistake	хато кардан	[χato kardan]
to manage, to run	сардорӣ кардан	[sardori: kardan]
to mean (signify)	маъно доштан	[ma'no doʃtan]
to mention (talk about)	гуфта гузаштан	[gufta guzaʃtan]
to miss (school, etc.)	набудан	[nabudan]
to notice (see)	дида мондан	[dida mondan]
to object (vi, vt)	зид баромадан	[zid baromadan]
to observe (see)	назорат кардан	[nazorat kardan]
to open (vt)	кушодан	[kuʃodan]
to order (meal, etc.)	супоридан	[suporidan]
to order (mil.)	фармон додан	[farmon dodan]
to own (possess)	соҳиб будан	[sohib budan]
to participate (vi)	иштирок кардан	[iʃtirok kardan]
to pay (vi, vt)	пул додан	[pul dodan]
to permit (vt)	иҷозат додан	[idʒozat dodan]
to plan (vt)	нақша кашидан	[naqʃa kaʃidan]
to play (children)	бозӣ кардан	[bozi: kardan]
to pray (vi, vt)	намоз хондан	[namoz χondan]
to prefer (vt)	бехтар донистан	[beχtar donistan]
to promise (vt)	ваъда додан	[va'da dodan]
to pronounce (vt)	талаффуз кардан	[talaffuz kardan]
to propose (vt)	таклиф кардан	[taklif kardan]
to punish (vt)	ҷазо додан	[dʒazo dodan]

16. The most important verbs. Part 4

to read (vi, vt)	хондан	[χondan]
to recommend (vt)	маслиҳат додан	[maslihat dodan]

to refuse (vi, vt)	рад кардан	[rad kardan]
to regret (be sorry)	таассуф хӯрдан	[taassuf χœrdan]
to rent (sth from sb)	ба иҷора гирифтан	[ba idʒora giriftan]

to repeat (say again)	такрор кардан	[takror kardan]
to reserve, to book	нигоҳ доштан	[nigoh doʃtan]
to run (vi)	давидан	[davidan]
to save (rescue)	наҷот додан	[nadʒot dodan]
to say (~ thank you)	гуфтан	[guftan]

to scold (vt)	дашном додан	[daʃnom dodan]
to see (vt)	дидан	[didan]
to sell (vt)	фурӯхтан	[furœχtan]
to send (vt)	ирсол кардан	[irsol kardan]
to shoot (vi)	тир задан	[tir zadan]

to shout (vi)	дод задан	[dod zadan]
to show (vt)	нишон додан	[niʃon dodan]
to sign (document)	имзо кардан	[imzo kardan]
to sit down (vi)	нишастан	[niʃastan]

to smile (vi)	табассум кардан	[tabassum kardan]
to speak (vi, vt)	гап задан	[gap zadan]
to steal (money, etc.)	дуздидан	[duzdidan]
to stop (for pause, etc.)	истодан	[istodan]
to stop (please ~ calling me)	бас кардан	[bas kardan]

to study (vt)	омӯхтан	[omœχtan]
to swim (vi)	шино кардан	[ʃino kardan]
to take (vt)	гирифтан	[giriftan]
to think (vi, vt)	фикр кардан	[fikr kardan]
to threaten (vt)	дӯғ задан	[dœʁ zadan]

to touch (with hands)	даст расондан	[dast rasondan]
to translate (vt)	тарҷума кардан	[tardʒuma kardan]
to trust (vt)	бовар кардан	[bovar kardan]
to try (attempt)	озмоиш кардан	[ozmoiʃ kardan]
to turn (e.g., ~ left)	гардонидан	[gardonidan]

to underestimate (vt)	хунукназари кардан	[χunuknazari: kardan]
to understand (vt)	фаҳмидан	[fahmidan]
to unite (vt)	якҷоя кардан	[jakdʒoja kardan]
to wait (vt)	поидан	[poidan]

to want (wish, desire)	хостан	[χostan]
to warn (vt)	танбеҳ додан	[tanbeh dodan]
to work (vi)	кор кардан	[kor kardan]
to write (vt)	навиштан	[naviʃtan]
to write down	навиштан	[naviʃtan]

TIME. CALENDAR

17. Weekdays

Monday	душанбе	[duʃanbe]
Tuesday	сешанбе	[seʃanbe]
Wednesday	чоршанбе	[tʃorʃanbe]
Thursday	панчшанбе	[pandʒʃanbe]
Friday	чумъа	[dʒum'a]
Saturday	шанбе	[ʃanbe]
Sunday	якшанбе	[jakʃanbe]
today (adv)	имрӯз	[imrœz]
tomorrow (adv)	пагоҳ, фардо	[pagoh], [fardo]
the day after tomorrow	пасфардо	[pasfardo]
yesterday (adv)	дирӯз, дина	[dirœz], [dina]
the day before yesterday	парирӯз	[parirœz]
day	рӯз	[rœz]
working day	рӯзи кор	[rœzi kor]
public holiday	рӯзи ид	[rœzi id]
day off	рӯзи истироҳат	[rœzi istirohat]
weekend	рӯзҳои истироҳат	[rœzhoi istirohat]
all day long	тамоми рӯз	[tamomi rœz]
the next day (adv)	рӯзи дигар	[rœzi digar]
two days ago	ду рӯз пеш	[du rœz peʃ]
the day before	як рӯз пеш	[jak rœz peʃ]
daily (adj)	ҳаррӯза	[harrœza]
every day (adv)	ҳар рӯз	[har rœz]
week	ҳафта	[hafta]
last week (adv)	ҳафтаи гузашта	[haftai guzaʃta]
next week (adv)	ҳафтаи оянда	[haftai ojanda]
weekly (adj)	ҳафтаина	[haftaina]
every week (adv)	ҳар ҳафта	[har hafta]
twice a week	ҳафтае ду маротиба	[haftae du marotiba]
every Tuesday	ҳар сешанбе	[har seʃanbe]

18. Hours. Day and night

morning	пагоҳӣ	[pagohi:]
in the morning	пагоҳирӯзӣ	[pagohirœzi:]
noon, midday	нисфи рӯз	[nisfi rœz]

in the afternoon	баъди пешин	[ba'di peʃin]
evening	бегоҳ, бегоҳирӯз	[begoh], [begohirœz]
in the evening	бегоҳӣ, бегоҳирӯзӣ	[begohi:], [begohirœzi:]
night	шаб	[ʃab]
at night	шабона	[ʃabona]
midnight	нисфи шаб	[nisfi ʃab]

second	сония	[sonija]
minute	дақиқа	[daqiqa]
hour	соат	[soat]
half an hour	нимсоат	[nimsoat]
a quarter-hour	чоряки соат	[tʃorjaki soat]
fifteen minutes	понздаҳ дақиқа	[ponzdah daqiqa]
24 hours	шабонарӯз	[ʃabonarœz]

sunrise	тулӯъ	[tulœ']
dawn	субҳидам	[subhidam]
early morning	субҳи барвақт	[subhi barvaqt]
sunset	ғуруби офтоб	[ʁurubi oftob]

early in the morning	субҳи барвақт	[subhi barvaqt]
this morning	имрӯз пагоҳӣ	[imrœz pagohi:]
tomorrow morning	пагоҳ саҳарӣ	[pagoh sahari:]

this afternoon	имрӯз	[imrœz]
in the afternoon	баъди пешин	[ba'di peʃin]
tomorrow afternoon	пагоҳ баъди пешин	[pagoh ba'di peʃin]

| tonight (this evening) | ҳамин бегоҳ | [hamin begoh] |
| tomorrow night | фардо бегоҳӣ | [fardo begohi:] |

at 3 o'clock sharp	расо соати се	[raso soati se]
about 4 o'clock	наздикии соати чор	[nazdiki:i soati tʃor]
by 12 o'clock	соатҳои дувоздаҳ	[soathoi duvozdah]

in 20 minutes	баъд аз бист дақиқа	[ba'd az bist daqiqa]
in an hour	баъд аз як соат	[ba'd az jak soat]
on time (adv)	дар вақташ	[dar vaqtaʃ]

a quarter of ...	понздаҳто кам	[ponzdahto kam]
within an hour	дар давоми як соат	[dar davomi jak soat]
every 15 minutes	ҳар понздаҳ дақиқа	[har ponzdah daqiqa]
round the clock	шабу рӯз	[ʃabu rœz]

19. Months. Seasons

January	январ	[janvar]
February	феврал	[fevral]
March	март	[mart]
April	апрел	[aprel]

May	май	[maj]
June	июн	[ijun]
July	июл	[ijul]
August	август	[avgust]
September	сентябр	[sentjabr]
October	октябр	[oktjabr]
November	ноябр	[nojabr]
December	декабр	[dekabr]
spring	баҳор, баҳорон	[bahor], [bahoron]
in spring	дар фасли баҳор	[dar fasli bahor]
spring (as adj)	баҳорӣ	[bahori:]
summer	тобистон	[tobiston]
in summer	дар тобистон	[dar tobiston]
summer (as adj)	тобистона	[tobistona]
fall	тирамоҳ	[tiramoh]
in fall	дар тирамоҳ	[dar tiramoh]
fall (as adj)	... и тирамоҳ	[i tiramoh]
winter	зимистон	[zimiston]
in winter	дар зимистон	[dar zimiston]
winter (as adj)	зимистонӣ,	[zimistoni:],
	... и зимистон	[i zimiston]
month	моҳ	[moh]
this month	ҳамин моҳ	[hamin moh]
next month	дар моҳи оянда	[dar mohi ojanda]
last month	дар моҳи гузашта	[dar mohi guzaʃta]
a month ago	як моҳ пеш	[jak moh peʃ]
in a month (a month later)	баъд аз як моҳ	[ba'd az jak moh]
in 2 months	баъд аз ду моҳ	[ba'd az du moh]
(2 months later)		
the whole month	тамоми моҳ	[tamomi moh]
all month long	тамоми моҳ	[tamomi moh]
monthly (~ magazine)	ҳармоҳа	[harmoha]
monthly (adv)	ҳар моҳ	[har moh]
every month	ҳар моҳ	[har moh]
twice a month	ду маротиба дар як моҳ	[du marotiba dar jak moh]
year	сол	[sol]
this year	ҳамин сол	[hamin sol]
next year	соли оянда	[soli ojanda]
last year	соли гузашта	[soli guzaʃta]
a year ago	як сол пеш	[jak sol peʃ]
in a year	баъд аз як сол	[ba'd az jak sol]
in two years	баъд аз ду сол	[ba'd az du sol]

| the whole year | тамоми сол | [tamomi sol] |
| all year long | як соли пурра | [jak soli purra] |

every year	ҳар сол	[har sol]
annual (adj)	ҳарсола	[harsola]
annually (adv)	ҳар сол	[har sol]
4 times a year	чор маротиба	[ʧor marotiba
	дар як сол	dar jak sol]

date (e.g., today's ~)	таърих, рӯз	[ta'riχ], [rœz]
date (e.g., ~ of birth)	сана	[sana]
calendar	тақвим, солнома	[taqvim], [solnoma]

half a year	ним сол	[nim sol]
six months	нимсола	[nimsola]
season (summer, etc.)	фасл	[fasl]
century	аср	[asr]

TRAVEL. HOTEL

20. Trip. Travel

tourism, travel	туризм, саёхат	[turizm], [sajɔχat]
tourist	саёхатчй	[sajɔhattʃi:]
trip, voyage	саёхат	[sajɔhat]
adventure	саргузашт	[sarguzaʃt]
trip, journey	сафар	[safar]
vacation	рухсатй	[ruχsati:]
to be on vacation	дар рухсатй будан	[dar ruχsati: budan]
rest	истирохат	[istirohat]
train	поезд, қатор	[poezd], [qator]
by train	бо қатора	[bo qatora]
airplane	хавопаймо	[havopajmo]
by airplane	бо хавопаймо	[bo havopajmo]
by car	бо мошин	[bo moʃin]
by ship	бо киштй	[bo kiʃti:]
luggage	бағоч, бор	[baʁɔdʒ], [bor]
suitcase	чомадон	[dʒomadon]
luggage cart	аробаи бағочкашй	[arobai boʁɔtʃkaʃi:]
passport	шиносома	[ʃinosnoma]
visa	виза	[viza]
ticket	билет	[bilet]
air ticket	чиптаи хавопаймо	[tʃiptai havopajmo]
guidebook	рохнома	[rohnoma]
map (tourist ~)	харита	[χarita]
area (rural ~)	чой, махал	[dʒɔj], [mahal]
place, site	чой	[dʒɔj]
exotica (n)	гароибот	[ʁaroibot]
exotic (adj)	… и гароиб	[i ʁaroib]
amazing (adj)	хайратангез	[hajratangez]
group	гурӯх	[gurœh]
excursion, sightseeing tour	экскурсия, саёхат	[ɛkskursija], [sajɔhat]
guide (person)	рохбари экскурсия	[rohbari ɛkskursija]

21. Hotel

hotel	меҳмонхона	[mehmonχona]
motel	меҳмонхона	[mehmonχona]
three-star (~ hotel)	се ситорадор	[se sitorador]
five-star	панҷ ситорадор	[pandʒ sitorador]
to stay (in a hotel, etc.)	фуромадан	[furomadan]
room	ҳуҷра	[hudʒra]
single room	ҳуҷраи якнафара	[hudʒrai jaknafara]
double room	ҳуҷраи дунафара	[hudʒrai dunafara]
to book a room	банд кардани ҳуҷра	[band kardani hudʒra]
half board	бо нимтаъминот	[bo nimta'minot]
full board	бо таъминоти пурра	[bo ta'minoti purra]
with bath	ваннадор	[vannador]
with shower	душдор	[duʃdor]
satellite television	телевизиони спутникӣ	[televizioni sputniki:]
air-conditioner	кондитсионер	[konditsioner]
towel	сачоқ	[satʃoq]
key	калид	[kalid]
administrator	маъмур, мудир	[ma'mur], [mudir]
chambermaid	пешхизмат	[peʃχizmat]
porter, bellboy	ҳаммол	[hammol]
doorman	дарбони меҳмонхона	[darboni mehmonχona]
restaurant	тарабхона	[tarabχona]
pub, bar	бар	[bar]
breakfast	ноништа	[noniʃta]
dinner	шом	[ʃom]
buffet	мизи шведӣ	[mizi ʃvedi:]
lobby	миёнсарой	[mijɔnsaroj]
elevator	лифт	[lift]
DO NOT DISTURB	ХАЛАЛ НАРАСОНЕД	[χalal narasoned]
NO SMOKING	ТАМОКУ НАКАШЕД!	[tamoku nakaʃed]

22. Sightseeing

monument	ҳайкал	[hajkal]
fortress	ҳисор	[hisor]
palace	қаср	[qasr]
castle	кӯшк	[kœʃk]
tower	манора, бурҷ	[manora], [burdʒ]
mausoleum	мавзолей, мақбара	[mavzolej], [maqbara]

architecture	меъморӣ	[me'mori:]
medieval (adj)	асримиёнагӣ	[əsrimijɔnagi:]
ancient (adj)	қадим	[qadim]
national (adj)	миллӣ	[milli:]
famous (monument, etc.)	маъруф	[ma'ruf]

tourist	саёхатчӣ	[sajɔhattʃi:]
guide (person)	роҳбалад	[rohbalad]
excursion, sightseeing tour	экскурсия	[ɛkskursija]
to show (vt)	нишон додан	[niʃon dodan]
to tell (vt)	нақл кардан	[naql kardan]

to find (vt)	ёфтан	[jɔftan]
to get lost (lose one's way)	роҳ гум кардан	[roh gum kardan]
map (e.g., subway ~)	нақша	[nakʃa]
map (e.g., city ~)	нақша	[naqʃa]

souvenir, gift	тӯҳфа	[tœhfa]
gift shop	мағозаи туҳфаҳо	[maʁozai tuhfahɔ]
to take pictures	сурат гирифтан	[surat giriftan]
to have one's picture taken	сурати худро гирондан	[surati χudro girondan]

TRANSPORTATION

23. Airport

airport	аэропорт	[aɛroport]
airplane	ҳавопаймо	[havopajmo]
airline	ширкати ҳавопаймой	[ʃirkati havopajmoi:]
air traffic controller	диспечер	[dispetʃer]
departure	парвоз	[parvoz]
arrival	парида омадан	[parida omadan]
to arrive (by plane)	парида омадан	[parida omadan]
departure time	вақти паридан	[vaqti paridan]
arrival time	вақти шиштан	[vaqti ʃiʃtan]
to be delayed	боздоштан	[bozdoʃtan]
flight delay	боздоштани парвоз	[bozdoʃtani parvoz]
information board	тахтаи ахборот	[taχtai aχborot]
information	ахборот	[aχborot]
to announce (vt)	эълон кардан	[ɛ'lon kardan]
flight (e.g., next ~)	сафар, рейс	[safar], [rejs]
customs	гумрукхона	[gumrukχona]
customs officer	гумрукчй	[gumruktʃi:]
customs declaration	декларатсияи гумрукй	[deklaratsijai gumruki:]
to fill out (vt)	пур кардан	[pur kardan]
to fill out the declaration	пур кардани декларатсия	[pur kardani deklaratsija]
passport control	назорати шиносномa	[nazorati ʃinosnoma]
luggage	багоҷ, бор	[baʁoʤ], [bor]
hand luggage	бори дастй	[bori dasti:]
luggage cart	аробаи богочкашй	[arobai boʁotʃkaʃi:]
landing	фуруд	[furud]
landing strip	хати нишаст	[χati niʃast]
to land (vi)	нишастан	[niʃastan]
airstairs	зинапояи киштй	[zinapojai kiʃti:]
check-in	бақайдгирй	[baqajdgiri:]
check-in counter	қатори бақайдгирй	[qatori baqajdgiri:]
to check-in (vi)	қайд кунондан	[qajd kunondan]
boarding pass	талони саворшавй	[taloni savorʃavi:]

departure gate	баромадан	[baromadan]
transit	транзит	[tranzit]
to wait (vt)	поидан	[poidan]
departure lounge	толори интизорӣ	[tolori intizori:]
to see off	гусел кардан	[gusel kardan]
to say goodbye	падруд гуфтан	[padrud guftan]

24. Airplane

airplane	ҳавопаймо	[havopajmo]
air ticket	чиптаи ҳавопаймо	[ʧiptai havopajmo]
airline	ширкати ҳавопаймой	[ʃirkati havopajmoi:]
airport	аэропорт	[aɛroport]
supersonic (adj)	фавқуссадо	[favqussado]

captain	фармондеҳи киштӣ	[farmondehi kiʃti:]
crew	экипаж	[ɛkipaʒ]
pilot	сарнишин	[sarniʃin]
flight attendant (fem.)	стюардесса	[stjuardessa]
navigator	штурман	[ʃturman]

wings	қанот	[qanot]
tail	дум	[dum]
cockpit	кабина	[kabina]
engine	муҳаррик	[muharrik]
undercarriage (landing gear)	шассӣ	[ʃassi:]
turbine	турбина	[turbina]

propeller	пропеллер	[propeller]
black box	қуттии сиёҳ	[qutti:i sijɔh]
yoke (control column)	суккон	[sukkon]
fuel	сӯзишворӣ	[sœziʃvori:]

safety card	дастурамали бехатарӣ	[dasturamali beχatari:]
oxygen mask	ниқоби ҳавои тоза	[niqobi havoi toza]
uniform	либоси расмӣ	[libosi rasmi:]
life vest	камзӯли наҷотдиҳанда	[kamzœli naʤotdihanda]
parachute	парашют	[paraʃjut]

takeoff	парвоз	[parvoz]
to take off (vi)	парвоз кардан	[parvoz kardan]
runway	хати парвоз	[χati parvoz]

visibility	софии ҳаво	[sofi:i havo]
flight (act of flying)	парвоз	[parvoz]
altitude	баландӣ	[balandi:]
air pocket	чоҳи ҳаво	[ʧohi havo]
seat	ҷой	[ʤoj]
headphones	гӯшак, гӯшпӯшак	[gœʃak], [gœʃpœʃak]

folding tray (tray table)	мизчаи вошаванда	[miztʃai voʃavanda]
airplane window	иллюминатор	[illjuminator]
aisle	гузаргоҳ	[guzargoh]

25. Train

train	поезд, қатор	[poezd], [qator]
commuter train	қатораи барқӣ	[qatorai barqi:]
express train	қатораи тезгард	[qatorai tezgard]
diesel locomotive	тепловоз	[teplovoz]
steam locomotive	паровоз	[parovoz]

| passenger car | вагон | [vagon] |
| dining car | вагон-ресторан | [vagon-restoran] |

rails	релсҳо	[relsho]
railroad	роҳи оҳан	[rohi ohan]
railway tie	шпала	[ʃpala]

platform (railway ~)	платформа	[platforma]
track (~ 1, 2, etc.)	роҳ	[roh]
semaphore	семафор	[semafor]
station	истгоҳ	[istgoh]

engineer (train driver)	мошинист	[moʃinist]
porter (of luggage)	ҳаммол	[hammol]
car attendant	роҳбалад	[rohbalad]
passenger	мусофир	[musofir]
conductor (ticket inspector)	нозир	[nozir]

| corridor (in train) | коридор | [koridor] |
| emergency brake | стоп-кран | [stop-kran] |

compartment	купе	[kupe]
berth	кат	[kat]
upper berth	кати боло	[kati bolo]
lower berth	кати поён	[kati pojon]
bed linen, bedding	чилдҳои болишту бистар	[dʒildhoi boliʃtu bistar]

ticket	билет	[bilet]
schedule	чадвал	[dʒadval]
information display	чадвал	[dʒadval]

to leave, to depart	дур шудан	[dur ʃudan]
departure (of train)	равон кардан	[ravon kardan]
to arrive (ab. train)	омадан	[omadan]
arrival	омадан	[omadan]
to arrive by train	бо қатора омадан	[bo qatora omadan]

| to get on the train | ба қатора нишастан | [ba qatora niʃastan] |
| to get off the train | фаромадан | [faromadan] |

| train wreck | садама | [sadama] |
| to derail (vi) | аз релс баромадан | [az rels baromadan] |

steam locomotive	паровоз	[parovoz]
stoker, fireman	алавмон	[alavmon]
firebox	оташдон	[otaʃdon]
coal	ангишт	[angiʃt]

26. Ship

| ship | киштӣ | [kiʃti:] |
| vessel | киштӣ | [kiʃti:] |

steamship	пароход	[paroχod]
riverboat	теплоход	[teploχod]
cruise ship	лайнер	[lajner]
cruiser	крейсер	[krejser]

yacht	яхта	[jaχta]
tugboat	таноби ядак	[tanobi jadak]
barge	баржа	[barʒa]
ferry	паром	[parom]

| sailing ship | киштии бодбондор | [kiʃti:i bodbondor] |
| brigantine | бригантина | [brigantina] |

| ice breaker | киштии яхшикан | [kiʃti:i jaχʃikan] |
| submarine | киштии зериобӣ | [kiʃti:i zeriobi:] |

boat (flat-bottomed ~)	қаиқ	[qaiq]
dinghy	қаиқ	[qaiq]
lifeboat	завраҡи наҷот	[zavraqi nadʒot]
motorboat	катер	[kater]

captain	капитан	[kapitan]
seaman	баҳрчӣ, маллоҳ	[bahrtʃi:], [malloh]
sailor	баҳрчӣ	[bahrtʃi:]
crew	экипаж	[ɛkipaʒ]

boatswain	ботсман	[botsman]
ship's boy	маллоҳбача	[mallohbatʃa]
cook	кок, ошпази киштӣ	[kok], [oʃpazi kiʃti:]
ship's doctor	духтури киштӣ	[duχturi kiʃti:]

deck	саҳни киштӣ	[sahni kiʃti:]
mast	сутуни киштӣ	[sutuni kiʃti:]
sail	бодбон	[bodbon]

hold	таҳхонаи киштӣ	[tahχonai kiʃti:]
bow (prow)	сари кишти	[sari kiʃti]
stern	думи киштӣ	[dumi kiʃti:]
oar	бели заврақ	[beli zavraq]
screw propeller	винт	[vint]

cabin	каюта	[kajuta]
wardroom	кают-компания	[kajut-kompanija]
engine room	шӯъбаи мошинхо	[ʃœ'bai moʃinho]
bridge	арша	[arʃa]
radio room	радиохона	[radioχona]
wave (radio)	мавҷ	[mavdʒ]
logbook	журнали киштӣ	[ʒurnali kiʃti:]

spyglass	дурбин	[durbin]
bell	ноқус, зангӯла	[noqus], [zangœla]
flag	байрак	[bajrak]

| hawser (mooring ~) | арғамчини ғафс | [arʁamtʃini ʁafs] |
| knot (bowline, etc.) | гиреҳ | [gireh] |

| deckrails | даста барои қапидан | [dasta baroi qapidan] |
| gangway | зинапоя | [zinapoja] |

anchor	лангар	[langar]
to weigh anchor	лангар бардоштан	[langar bardoʃtan]
to drop anchor	лангар андохтан	[langar andoχtan]
anchor chain	занҷири лангар	[zandʒiri langar]

port (harbor)	бандар	[bandar]
quay, wharf	ҷои киштибандӣ	[dʒoi kiʃtibandi:]
to berth (moor)	ба соҳил овардан	[ba sohil ovardan]
to cast off	ҳаракат кардан	[harakat kardan]

trip, voyage	саёҳат	[sajɔhat]
cruise (sea trip)	круиз	[kruiz]
course (route)	самт	[samt]
route (itinerary)	маршрут	[marʃrut]

fairway	маъбар	[ma'bar]
(safe water channel)		
shallows	тунукоба	[tunukoba]
to run aground	ба тунукоба шиштан	[ba tunukoba ʃiʃtan]

storm	тӯфон, бӯрои	[tœfon], [bœroi]
signal	бонг, ишорат	[bong], [iʃorat]
to sink (vi)	ғарк шудан	[ʁark ʃudan]
Man overboard!	Одам дар об!	[odam dar ob]
SOS (distress signal)	SOS	[sos]
ring buoy	чамбари начот	[tʃambari nadʒot]

CITY

27. Urban transportation

bus	автобус	[avtobus]
streetcar	трамвай	[tramvaj]
trolley bus	троллейбус	[trollejbus]
route (of bus, etc.)	маршрут	[marʃrut]
number (e.g., bus ~)	рақам	[raqam]
to go by …	савор будан	[savor budan]
to get on (~ the bus)	савор шудан	[savor ʃudan]
to get off …	фуромадан	[furomadan]
stop (e.g., bus ~)	истгоҳ	[istgoh]
next stop	истгоҳи дигар	[istgohi digar]
terminus	истгоҳи охирон	[istgohi oxiron]
schedule	ҷадвал	[dʒadval]
to wait (vt)	поидан	[poidan]
ticket	билет	[bilet]
fare	арзиши чипта	[arziʃi tʃipta]
cashier (ticket seller)	кассир	[kassir]
ticket inspection	назорат	[nazorat]
ticket inspector	нозир	[nozir]
to be late (for …)	дер мондан	[der mondan]
to miss (~ the train, etc.)	дер мондан	[der mondan]
to be in a hurry	шитоб кардан	[ʃitob kardan]
taxi, cab	такси	[taksi]
taxi driver	таксичӣ	[taksitʃi:]
by taxi	дар такси	[dar taksi]
taxi stand	истгоҳи таксӣ	[istgohi taksi:]
to call a taxi	даъват кардани таксӣ	[da'vat kardani taksi:]
to take a taxi	такси гирифтан	[taksi giriftan]
traffic	ҳаракат дар кӯча	[harakat dar kœtʃa]
traffic jam	пробка	[probka]
rush hour	час пик	[tʃas pik]
to park (vi)	ҷой кардан	[dʒoj kardan]
to park (vt)	ҷой кардан	[dʒoj kardan]
parking lot	истгоҳ	[istgoh]
subway	метро	[metro]
station	истгоҳ	[istgoh]

to take the subway	бо метро рафтан	[bo metro raftan]
train	поезд, қатор	[poezd], [qator]
train station	вокзал	[vokzal]

28. City. Life in the city

city, town	шаҳр	[ʃahr]
capital city	пойтахт	[pojtaχt]
village	деҳа, деҳ	[deha], [deh]

city map	нақшаи шаҳр	[naqʃai ʃahr]
downtown	маркази шаҳр	[markazi ʃahr]
suburb	шаҳрча	[ʃahrtʃa]
suburban (adj)	наздишаҳрӣ	[nazdiʃahri:]

outskirts	атроф, канор	[atrof], [kanor]
environs (suburbs)	атрофи шаҳр	[atrofi ʃahr]
city block	квартал, маҳалла	[kvartal], [mahalla]
residential block (area)	маҳаллаи истиқоматӣ	[mahallai istiqomati:]

traffic	ҳаракат дар кӯча	[harakat dar kœtʃa]
traffic lights	чароғи раҳнамо	[tʃaroʁi rahnamo]
public transportation	нақлиёти шаҳрӣ	[naqlijoti ʃahri:]
intersection	чорраҳа	[tʃorraha]

crosswalk	гузаргоҳи пиёдагардон	[guzargohi pijodagardon]
pedestrian underpass	гузаргоҳи зеризаминӣ	[guzargohi zerizamini:]
to cross (~ the street)	гузаштан	[guzaʃtan]
pedestrian	пиёдагард	[pijodagard]
sidewalk	пиёдараҳа	[pijodaraha]

bridge	пул, кӯпрук	[pul], [kœpruk]
embankment (river walk)	соҳил	[sohil]
fountain	фаввора	[favvora]

allée (garden walkway)	кӯчабоғ	[kœtʃaboʁ]
park	боғ	[boʁ]
boulevard	кӯчабоғ, гулгашт	[kœtʃaboʁ], [gulgaʃt]
square	майдон	[majdon]
avenue (wide street)	хиёбон	[χijobon]
street	кӯча	[kœtʃa]
side street	тангкӯча	[tangkœtʃa]
dead end	кӯчаи бумбаста	[kœtʃai bumbasta]

house	хона	[χona]
building	бино	[bino]
skyscraper	иморати осмонхарош	[imorati osmonχaroʃ]

| facade | намо | [namo] |
| roof | бом | [bom] |

window	тиреза	[tireza]
arch	равоқ, тоқ	[ravoq], [toq]
column	сутун	[sutun]
corner	бурчак	[burtʃak]

store window	витрина	[vitrina]
signboard (store sign, etc.)	лавҳа	[lavha]
poster	эълоннома	[ɛ'lonnoma]
advertising poster	плакати реклама	[plakati reklama]
billboard	лавҳаи эълонҳо	[lavhai ɛ'lonho]

garbage, trash	ахлот, хокрӯба	[aχlot], [χokrœba]
trashcan (public ~)	ахлотқуттӣ	[aχlotqutti:]
to litter (vi)	ифлос кардан	[iflos kardan]
garbage dump	партовгоҳ	[partovgoh]

phone booth	будкаи телефон	[budkai telefon]
lamppost	сутуни фонус	[sutuni fonus]
bench (park ~)	нимкат	[nimkat]

police officer	полис	[polis]
police	полис	[polis]
beggar	гадо	[gado]
homeless (n)	бехона	[beχona]

29. Urban institutions

store	магазин	[magazin]
drugstore, pharmacy	дорухона	[doruχona]
eyeglass store	оптика	[optika]
shopping mall	маркази савдо	[markazi savdo]
supermarket	супермаркет	[supermarket]

bakery	дӯкони нонфурӯшӣ	[dœkoni nonfurœʃi:]
baker	нонвой	[nonvoj]
pastry shop	қаннодӣ	[qannodi:]
grocery store	дӯкони баққолӣ	[dœkoni baqqoli:]
butcher shop	дӯкони гӯштфурӯшӣ	[dœkoni gœʃtfurœʃi:]

| produce store | дӯкони сабзавот | [dœkoni sabzavot] |
| market | бозор | [bozor] |

coffee house	қаҳвахона	[qahvaχona]
restaurant	тарабхона	[tarabχona]
pub, bar	пивохона	[pivoχona]
pizzeria	питсерия	[pitserija]

hair salon	сартарошхона	[sartaroʃχona]
post office	пӯшта	[pœʃta]
dry cleaners	козургарии химиявӣ	[kozurgari:i χimijavi:]

photo studio	суратгирхона	[suratgirχona]
shoe store	магазини пойафзолфурӯшӣ	[magazini pojafzolfurœʃiː]
bookstore	мағозаи китоб	[maʁozai kitob]
sporting goods store	мағозаи варзишӣ	[maʁozai varziʃiː]
clothes repair shop	таъмири либос	[taʔmiri libos]
formal wear rental	кирояи либос	[kirojai libos]
video rental store	кирояи филмҳо	[kirojai filmho]
circus	сирк	[sirk]
zoo	боғи ҳайвонот	[boʁi hajvonot]
movie theater	кинотеатр	[kinoteatr]
museum	осорхона	[osorχona]
library	китобхона	[kitobχona]
theater	театр	[teatr]
opera (opera house)	опера	[opera]
nightclub	клуби шабона	[klubi ʃabona]
casino	казино	[kazino]
mosque	масҷид	[masdʒid]
synagogue	каниса	[kanisa]
cathedral	собор	[sobor]
temple	ибодатгоҳ	[ibodatgoh]
church	калисо	[kaliso]
college	институт	[institut]
university	университет	[universitet]
school	мактаб	[maktab]
prefecture	префектура	[prefektura]
city hall	мэрия	[mɛrija]
hotel	меҳмонхона	[mehmonχona]
bank	банк	[bank]
embassy	сафорат	[saforat]
travel agency	турагенство	[turagenstvo]
information office	бюрои справкадиҳӣ	[bjuroi spravkadihiː]
currency exchange	нуқтаи мубодила	[nuqtai mubodila]
subway	метро	[metro]
hospital	касалхона	[kasalχona]
gas station	нуқтаи фурӯши сӯзишворӣ	[nuqtai furœʃi sœziʃvoriː]
parking lot	истгоҳи мошинҳо	[istgohi moʃinho]

30. Signs

signboard (store sign, etc.)	лавҳа	[lavha]
notice (door sign, etc.)	хат, навиштаҷот	[χat], [naviʃtadʒot]

poster	плакат	[plakat]
direction sign	аломат, нишона	[alomat], [niʃona]
arrow (sign)	аломати тир	[alomati tir]

caution	огоҳӣ	[ogohi:]
warning sign	огоҳӣ	[ogohi:]
to warn (vt)	танбеҳ додан	[tanbeh dodan]

rest day (weekly ~)	рӯзи истироҳат	[rœzi istirohat]
timetable (schedule)	ҷадвал	[dʒadval]
opening hours	соати корӣ	[soati kori:]

WELCOME!	ХУШ ОМАДЕД!	[xuʃ omaded]
ENTRANCE	ДАРОМАД	[daromad]
EXIT	БАРОМАД	[baromad]

PUSH	АЗ ХУД	[az xud]
PULL	БА ХУД	[ba xud]
OPEN	КУШОДА	[kuʃoda]
CLOSED	ПӮШИДА	[pœʃida]

| WOMEN | БАРОИ ЗАНОН | [baroi zanon] |
| MEN | БАРОИ МАРДОН | [baroi mardon] |

DISCOUNTS	ТАХФИФ	[taxfif]
SALE	АРЗОНФУРӮШӢ	[arzonfurœʃi:]
NEW!	МОЛИ НАВ!	[moli nav]
FREE	БЕПУЛ	[bepul]

ATTENTION!	ДИҚҚАТ!	[diqqat]
NO VACANCIES	ҶОЙ НЕСТ	[dʒoj nest]
RESERVED	БАНД АСТ	[band ast]

| ADMINISTRATION | МАЪМУРИЯТ | [ma'murijat] |
| STAFF ONLY | ФАҚАТ БАРОИ КОРМАНДОН | [faqat baroi kormandon] |

BEWARE OF THE DOG!	САГИ ГАЗАНДА	[sagi gazanda]
NO SMOKING	ТАМОКУ НАКАШЕД!	[tamoku nakaʃed]
DO NOT TOUCH!	ДАСТ НАРАСОНЕД!	[dast narasoned]

DANGEROUS	ХАТАРНОК	[xatarnok]
DANGER	ХАТАР	[xatar]
HIGH VOLTAGE	ШИДДАТИ БАЛАНД	[ʃiddati baland]
NO SWIMMING!	ОББОЗӢ КАРДАН МАНЪ АСТ	[obbozi: kardan man' ast]
OUT OF ORDER	КОР НАМЕКУНАД	[kor namekunad]

FLAMMABLE	ОТАШАНГЕЗ	[otaʃangez]
FORBIDDEN	МАНЪ АСТ	[man' ast]
NO TRESPASSING!	ДАРОМАД МАНЪ АСТ	[daromad man' ast]
WET PAINT	РАНГ КАРДА ШУДААСТ	[rang karda ʃudaast]

31. Shopping

to buy (purchase)	харидан	[χaridan]
purchase	харид	[χarid]
to go shopping	харид кардан	[χarid kardan]
shopping	шопинг	[ʃoping]
to be open (ab. store)	кушода будан	[kuʃoda budan]
to be closed	маҳкам будан	[mahkam budan]
footwear, shoes	пойафзол	[pojafzol]
clothes, clothing	либос	[libos]
cosmetics	косметика	[kosmetika]
food products	озуқаворӣ	[ozuqavori:]
gift, present	тӯҳфа	[tœhfa]
salesman	фурӯш	[furœʃ]
saleswoman	фурӯш	[furœʃ]
check out, cash desk	касса	[kassa]
mirror	оина	[oina]
counter (store ~)	пешдӯкон	[peʃdœkon]
fitting room	ҷои пӯшида дидани либос	[dʒoi pœʃida didani libos]
to try on	пӯшида дидан	[pœʃida didan]
to fit (ab. dress, etc.)	мувофиқ омадан	[muvofiq omadan]
to like (I like …)	форидан	[foridan]
price	нарх	[narχ]
price tag	нархнома	[narχnoma]
to cost (vt)	арзидан	[arzidan]
How much?	Чанд пул?	[tʃand pul]
discount	тахфиф	[taχfif]
inexpensive (adj)	арзон	[arzon]
cheap (adj)	арзон	[arzon]
expensive (adj)	қимат	[qimat]
It's expensive	Ин қимат аст	[in qimat ast]
rental (n)	кироя	[kiroja]
to rent (~ a tuxedo)	насия гирифтан	[nasija giriftan]
credit (trade credit)	қарз	[qarz]
on credit (adv)	кредит гирифтан	[kredit giriftan]

CLOTHING & ACCESSORIES

32. Outerwear. Coats

clothes	либос	[libos]
outerwear	либоси боло	[libosi bolo]
winter clothing	либоси зимистонӣ	[libosi zimistoni:]
coat (overcoat)	палто	[palto]
fur coat	пӯстин	[pœstin]
fur jacket	нимпӯстин	[nimpœstin]
down coat	пуховик	[puxovik]
jacket (e.g., leather ~)	куртка	[kurtka]
raincoat (trenchcoat, etc.)	боронӣ	[boroni:]
waterproof (adj)	обногузар	[obnoguzar]

33. Men's & women's clothing

shirt (button shirt)	курта	[kurta]
pants	шим, шалвор	[ʃim], [ʃalvor]
jeans	шими ҷинс	[ʃimi dʒins]
suit jacket	пиҷак	[pidʒak]
suit	костюм	[kostjum]
dress (frock)	куртаи заннона	[kurtai zannona]
skirt	юбка	[jubka]
blouse	блузка	[bluzka]
knitted jacket (cardigan, etc.)	кофтаи бофта	[koftai bofta]
jacket (of woman's suit)	жакет	[ʒaket]
T-shirt	футболка	[futbolka]
shorts (short trousers)	шортик	[ʃortik]
tracksuit	либоси варзишӣ	[libosi varziʃi:]
bathrobe	халат	[xalat]
pajamas	пижама	[piʒama]
sweater	свитер	[sviter]
pullover	пуловер	[pulover]
vest	камзӯл	[kamzœl]
tailcoat	фрак	[frak]
tuxedo	смокинг	[smoking]

uniform	либоси расмӣ	[libosi rasmi:]
workwear	либоси корӣ	[libosi kori:]
overalls	комбинезон	[kombinezon]
coat (e.g., doctor's smock)	халат	[xalat]

34. Clothing. Underwear

underwear	либоси таг	[libosi tag]
boxers, briefs	турсуки мардона	[tursuki mardona]
panties	турсуки занона	[tursuki zanona]
undershirt (A-shirt)	майка	[majka]
socks	пайпоқ	[pajpoq]

nightgown	куртаи хоб	[kurtai xob]
bra	синабанд	[sinaband]
knee highs (knee-high socks)	ҷуроби кутоҳ	[dʒurobi kutoh]
pantyhose	колготка	[kolgotka]
stockings (thigh highs)	ҷуроби дароз	[tʃurobi daroz]
bathing suit	либоси оббозӣ	[libosi obbozi:]

35. Headwear

hat	кулоҳ, телпак	[kuloh], [telpak]
fedora	шляпаи моҳутӣ	[ʃljapai mohuti:]
baseball cap	бейсболка	[bejsbolka]
flatcap	кепка	[kepka]

beret	берет	[beret]
hood	либоси кулоҳдор	[libosi kulohdor]
panama hat	панамка	[panamka]
knit cap (knitted hat)	шапкаи бофтагӣ	[ʃapkai boftagi:]

headscarf	рӯймол	[rœjmol]
women's hat	кулоҳча	[kulohtʃa]
hard hat	тоскулоҳ	[toskuloh]
garrison cap	пилотка	[pilotka]
helmet	хӯд	[xœd]

| derby | дегчакулох | [degtʃakuloχ] |
| top hat | силиндр | [silindr] |

36. Footwear

| footwear | пойафзол | [pojafzol] |
| shoes (men's shoes) | патинка | [patinka] |

shoes (women's shoes)	кафш, туфли	[kafʃ], [tufli]
boots (e.g., cowboy ~)	мӯза	[mœza]
slippers	шиппак	[ʃippak]

tennis shoes (e.g., Nike ~)	крассовка	[krassovka]
sneakers (e.g., Converse ~)	кетй	[keti:]
sandals	сандал	[sandal]

cobbler (shoe repairer)	мӯзадӯз	[mœzadœz]
heel	пошна	[poʃna]
pair (of shoes)	чуфт	[dʒuft]

shoestring	бандак	[bandak]
to lace (vt)	бандак гузарондан	[bandak guzarondan]
shoehorn	кафчаи кафшпӯшй	[kaftʃai kafʃpœʃi:]
shoe polish	креми пойафзол	[kremi pojafzol]

37. Personal accessories

gloves	дастпӯшак	[dastpœʃak]
mittens	дастпӯшаки бепанча	[dastpœʃaki bepandʒa]
scarf (muffler)	гарданпеч	[gardanpetʃ]

glasses (eyeglasses)	айнак	[ajnak]
frame (eyeglass ~)	чанбарак	[tʃanbarak]
umbrella	соябон, чатр	[sojabon], [tʃatr]
walking stick	чӯб	[tʃœb]

hairbrush	чӯткаи мӯйсар	[tʃœtkai mœjsar]
fan	бодбезак	[bodbezak]

tie (necktie)	галстук	[galstuk]
bow tie	галстук-шапарак	[galstuk-ʃaparak]

suspenders	шалворбанди китфй	[ʃalvorbandi kitfi:]
handkerchief	дастрӯймол	[dastrœjmol]

comb	шона	[ʃona]
barrette	сарсӯзан, бандак	[sarsœzan], [bandak]

hairpin	санчак	[sandʒak]
buckle	сагаки тасма	[sagaki tasma]

belt	тасма	[tasma]
shoulder strap	тасма	[tasma]

bag (handbag)	сумка	[sumka]
purse	сумка	[sumka]
backpack	борхалта	[borχalta]

38. Clothing. Miscellaneous

fashion	мод	[mod]
in vogue (adj)	модшуда	[modʃuda]
fashion designer	тарҳсоз	[tarhsoz]
collar	гиребон, ёқа	[girebon], [jɔqa]
pocket	киса	[kisa]
pocket (as adj)	... и киса	[i kisa]
sleeve	остин	[ostin]
hanging loop	банди либос	[bandi libos]
fly (on trousers)	чоки пеши шим	[tʃoki peʃi ʃim]
zipper (fastener)	занҷирак	[zandʒirak]
fastener	гиреҳбанд	[girehband]
button	тугма	[tugma]
buttonhole	банди тугма	[bandi tugma]
to come off (ab. button)	канда шудан	[kanda ʃudan]
to sew (vi, vt)	дӯхтан	[dœxtan]
to embroider (vi, vt)	гулдӯзй кардан	[guldœzi: kardan]
embroidery	гулдӯзй	[guldœzi:]
sewing needle	сӯзани чокдӯзи	[sœzani tʃokdœzi]
thread	ресмон	[resmon]
seam	чок	[tʃok]
to get dirty (vi)	олуда шудан	[oluda ʃudan]
stain (mark, spot)	доғ, лакка	[doʁ], [lakka]
to crease, crumple (vi)	ғичим шудан	[ʁidʒim ʃudan]
to tear, to rip (vt)	дwaррондан	[darrondan]
clothes moth	куя	[kuja]

39. Personal care. Cosmetics

toothpaste	хамираи дандон	[xamirai dandon]
toothbrush	чӯткаи дандоншӯй	[tʃœtkai dandonʃœi:]
to brush one's teeth	дандон шустан	[dandon ʃustan]
razor	ришгирак	[riʃgirak]
shaving cream	креми ришгирй	[kremi riʃgiri:]
to shave (vi)	риш гирифтан	[riʃ giriftan]
soap	собун	[sobun]
shampoo	шампун	[ʃampun]
scissors	кайчй	[kajtʃi:]
nail file	тарошаи нохунхо	[taroʃai noxunho]
nail clippers	анбӯрча барои нохунхо	[anbœrtʃa baroi noxunho]
tweezers	мӯйчинак	[mœjtʃinak]

cosmetics	косметика	[kosmetika]
face mask	ниқоби косметикй	[niqobi kosmetiki:]
manicure	нохунорой	[noxunoroi:]
to have a manicure	нохун оростан	[noxun orostan]
pedicure	ороиши нохунҳои пой	[oroiʃi noxunhoi poj]

make-up bag	косметичка	[kosmetitʃka]
face powder	сафеда	[safeda]
powder compact	қуттии упо	[qutti:i upo]
blusher	сурхй	[surxi:]

toilet water (lotion)	атр	[atr]
lotion	оби мушкин	[obi muʃkin]
cologne	атр	[atr]

eyeshadow	тен барои пилкҳои чашм	[ten baroi pilkhoi tʃaʃm]
eyeliner	қалами чашм	[qalami tʃaʃm]
mascara	туш барои мижаҳо	[tuʃ baroi miʒaho]

lipstick	лабсурхкунак	[labsurxkunak]
nail polish, enamel	лаки нохун	[laki noxun]
hair spray	лаки мӯйсар	[laki mœjsar]
deodorant	дезодорант	[dezodorant]

cream	крем, равғани рӯй	[krem], [ravʁani rœj]
face cream	креми рӯй	[kremi rœj]
hand cream	креми даст	[kremi dast]
anti-wrinkle cream	креми зиддиожанг	[kremi ziddioʒang]
day cream	креми рӯзона	[kremi rœzona]
night cream	креми шабона	[kremi ʃabona]
day (as adj)	рӯзона, ~и рӯз	[rœzona], [~i rœz]
night (as adj)	шабона, ... и шаб	[ʃabona], [i ʃab]

tampon	тампон	[tampon]
toilet paper (toilet roll)	коғази хоҷатхона	[koʁazi xoʤatxona]
hair dryer	мӯхушккунак	[mœxuʃkkunak]

40. Watches. Clocks

watch (wristwatch)	соати дастй	[soati dasti:]
dial	лавҳаи соат	[lavhai soat]
hand (of clock, watch)	акрабак	[akrabak]
metal watch band	дастпона	[dastpona]
watch strap	банди соат	[bandi soat]

battery	батареяча, батарейка	[batarejatʃa], [batarejka]
to be dead (battery)	холй шудааст	[xoli: ʃudaast]
to change a battery	иваз кардани батаре	[ivaz kardani batare]
to run fast	пеш меравад	[peʃ meravad]

to run slow	ақиб мондан	[aqib mondan]
wall clock	соати деворӣ	[soati devori:]
hourglass	соати регӣ	[soati regi:]
sundial	соати офтобӣ	[soati oftobi:]
alarm clock	соати рӯимизии зангдор	[soati rœimizi:i zangdor]
watchmaker	соатсоз	[soatsoz]
to repair (vt)	таъмир кардан	[ta'mir kardan]

EVERYDAY EXPERIENCE

41. Money

money	пул	[pul]
currency exchange	мубодила, иваз	[mubodila], [ivaz]
exchange rate	қурб	[qurb]
ATM	банкомат	[bankomat]
coin	танга	[tanga]
dollar	доллар	[dollar]
lira	лираи италиявӣ	[lirai italijavi:]
Deutschmark	маркаи олмонӣ	[markai olmoni:]
franc	франк	[frank]
pound sterling	фунт стерлинг	[funt sterling]
yen	иена	[iena]
debt	қарз	[qarz]
debtor	қарздор	[qarzdor]
to lend (money)	қарз додан	[qarz dodan]
to borrow (vi, vt)	қарз гирифтан	[qarz giriftan]
bank	банк	[bank]
account	ҳисоб	[hisob]
to deposit (vt)	гузарондан	[guzarondan]
to deposit into the account	ба суратҳисоб гузарондан	[ba surathisob guzarondan]
to withdraw (vt)	аз суратҳисоб гирифтан	[az surathisob giriftan]
credit card	корти кредитӣ	[korti krediti:]
cash	пули нақд, нақдина	[puli naqd], [naqdina]
check	чек	[tʃek]
to write a check	чек навиштан	[tʃek naviʃtan]
checkbook	дафтарчаи чек	[daftartʃai tʃek]
wallet	ҳамён	[hamjɔn]
change purse	ҳамён	[hamjɔn]
safe	сейф	[sejf]
heir	меросхӯр	[merosχœr]
inheritance	мерос	[meros]
fortune (wealth)	дорой	[doroi:]
lease	иҷора	[idʒora]
rent (money)	ҳаққи манзил	[haqqi manzil]

to rent (sth from sb)	ба иҷора гирифтан	[ba idʒora giriftan]
price	нарх	[narχ]
cost	арзиш	[arziʃ]
sum	маблағ	[mablaʁ]
to spend (vt)	сарф кардан	[sarf kardan]
expenses	харҷ, ҳазина	[χardʒ], [hazina]
to economize (vi, vt)	сарфа кардан	[sarfa kardan]
economical	сарфакор	[sarfakor]
to pay (vi, vt)	пул додан	[pul dodan]
payment	пардохт	[pardoχt]
change (give the ~)	бақияи пул	[baqijai pul]
tax	налог, андоз	[nalog], [andoz]
fine	ҷарима	[dʒarima]
to fine (vt)	ҷарима андохтан	[dʒarima andoχtan]

42. Post. Postal service

post office	почта	[potʃta]
mail (letters, etc.)	почта	[potʃta]
mailman	хаткашон	[χatkaʃon]
opening hours	соати корӣ	[soati kori:]
letter	мактуб	[maktub]
registered letter	хати супориш	[χati suporiʃi:]
postcard	рукъа	[ruq'a]
telegram	барқия	[barqija]
package (parcel)	равонак	[ravonak]
money transfer	пули фиристодашуда	[puli firistodaʃuda]
to receive (vt)	гирифтан	[giriftan]
to send (vt)	ирсол кардан	[irsol kardan]
sending	ирсол	[irsol]
address	адрес, унвон	[adres], [unvon]
ZIP code	индекси почта	[indeksi potʃta]
sender	ирсолкунанда	[irsolkunanda]
receiver	гиранда	[giranda]
name (first name)	ном	[nom]
surname (last name)	фамилия	[familija]
postage rate	таърифа	[ta'rifa]
standard (adj)	муқаррарӣ	[muqarrari:]
economical (adj)	камхарҷ	[kamχardʒ]
weight	вазн	[vazn]
to weigh (~ letters)	баркашидан	[barkaʃidan]

envelope	конверт	[konvert]
postage stamp	марка	[marka]
to stamp an envelope	марка часпонидан	[marka tʃasponidan]

43. Banking

| bank | банк | [bank] |
| branch (of bank, etc.) | шӯъба | [ʃœ'ba] |

| bank clerk, consultant | мушовир | [muʃovir] |
| manager (director) | идоракунанда | [idorakunanda] |

bank account	ҳисоб	[hisob]
account number	рақами суратҳисоб	[raqami surathisob]
checking account	ҳисоби ҷорй	[hisobi dʒori:]
savings account	суратҳисоби ҷамъшаванда	[surathisobi dʒam'ʃavanda]

to open an account	суратҳисоб кушодан	[surathisob kuʃodan]
to close the account	бастани суратҳисоб	[bastani surathisob]
to deposit into the account	ба суратҳисоб гузарондан	[ba surathisob guzarondan]
to withdraw (vt)	аз суратҳисоб гирифтан	[az surathisob giriftan]

deposit	амонат	[amonat]
to make a deposit	маблағ гузоштан	[mablaʁ guzoʃtan]
wire transfer	интиқоли маблағ	[intiqoli mablaʁ]
to wire, to transfer	интиқол додан	[intiqol dodan]
sum	маблағ	[mablaʁ]
How much?	Чй қадар?	[tʃi: qadar]

| signature | имзо | [imzo] |
| to sign (vt) | имзо кардан | [imzo kardan] |

credit card	корти кредитй	[korti krediti:]
code (PIN code)	рамз, код	[ramz], [kod]
credit card number	рақами корти кредитй	[raqami korti krediti:]
ATM	банкомат	[bankomat]

check	чек	[tʃek]
to write a check	чек навиштан	[tʃek naviʃtan]
checkbook	дафтарчаи чек	[daftartʃai tʃek]

loan (bank ~)	қарз	[qarz]
to apply for a loan	барои кредит мурочиат кардан	[baroi kredit murodʒiat kardan]
to get a loan	кредит гирифтан	[kredit giriftan]
to give a loan	кредит додан	[kredit dodan]
guarantee	кафолат, замонат	[kafolat], [zamonat]

44. Telephone. Phone conversation

telephone	телефон	[telefon]
cell phone	телефони мобилӣ	[telefoni mobili:]
answering machine	худчавобгӯ	[χuddʒavobgœ]
to call (by phone)	телефон кардан	[telefon kardan]
phone call	занг	[zang]
to dial a number	гирифтани рақамхо	[giriftani raqamho]
Hello!	алло, ҳа	[allo], [ha]
to ask (vt)	пурсидан	[pursidan]
to answer (vi, vt)	чавоб додан	[dʒavob dodan]
to hear (vt)	шунидан	[ʃunidan]
well (adv)	хуб, наӻз	[χub], [naʁz]
not well (adv)	бад	[bad]
noises (interference)	садохои бегона	[sadohoi begona]
receiver	гӯшак	[giːʃak]
to pick up (~ the phone)	бардоштани гӯшак	[bardoʃtani gœʃak]
to hang up (~ the phone)	мондани гӯшак	[mondani gœʃak]
busy (engaged)	банд	[band]
to ring (ab. phone)	занг задан	[zang zadan]
telephone book	китоби телефон	[kitobi telefon]
local (adj)	маҳаллӣ	[mahalli:]
local call	занги маҳаллӣ	[zangi mahalli:]
long distance (~ call)	байнишаҳрӣ	[bajniʃahri:]
long-distance call	занги байнишаҳрӣ	[zangi bajniʃahri:]
international (adj)	байналхалқӣ	[bajnalχalqi:]

45. Cell phone

cell phone	телефони мобилӣ	[telefoni mobili:]
display	дисплей	[displej]
button	тугмача	[tugmatʃa]
SIM card	сим-корт	[sim-kort]
battery	батарея	[batareja]
to be dead (battery)	бе заряд шудан	[be zarjad ʃudan]
charger	асбоби барқпуркунанда	[asbobi barqpurkunanda]
menu	меню	[menju]
settings	соз кардан	[soz kardan]
tune (melody)	оҳанг	[ohang]
to select (vt)	интихоб кардан	[intiχob kardan]
calculator	ҳисобкунак	[hisobkunak]

voice mail	худҷавобгӯ	[χudʤavobgœ]
alarm clock	соати рӯимизии зангдор	[soati rœimizi:i zangdor]
contacts	китоби телефон	[kitobi telefon]
SMS (text message)	СМС-хабар	[sms-χabar]
subscriber	муштарй	[muʃtari:]

46. Stationery

ballpoint pen	ручкаи саққочадор	[rutʃkai saqqotʃador]
fountain pen	парқалам	[parqalam]
pencil	қалам	[qalam]
highlighter	маркер	[marker]
felt-tip pen	фломастер	[flomaster]
notepad	блокнот, дафтари ёддошт	[bloknot], [daftari jɔddoʃt]
agenda (diary)	рӯзнома	[rœznoma]
ruler	ҷадвал	[ʤadval]
calculator	ҳисобкунак	[hisobkunak]
eraser	ластик	[lastik]
thumbtack	кнопка	[knopka]
paper clip	скрепка	[skrepka]
glue	елим, шилм	[elim], [ʃilm]
stapler	степлер	[stepler]
pencil sharpener	чарх	[tʃarχ]

47. Foreign languages

language	забон	[zabon]
foreign (adj)	хориҷй	[χoriʤi:]
foreign language	забони хориҷй	[zaboni χoriʤi:]
to study (vt)	омӯхтан	[omœχtan]
to learn (language, etc.)	омӯхтан	[omœχtan]
to read (vi, vt)	хондан	[χondan]
to speak (vi, vt)	гап задан	[gap zadan]
to understand (vt)	фаҳмидан	[fahmidan]
to write (vt)	навиштан	[naviʃtan]
fast (adv)	босуръат	[bosur'at]
slowly (adv)	оҳиста	[ohista]
fluently (adv)	озодона	[ozodona]
rules	қоидаҳо	[qoidaho]

grammar	грамматика	[grammatika]
vocabulary	лексика	[leksika]
phonetics	савтиёт	[savtijɔt]
textbook	китоби дарсӣ	[kitobi darsi:]
dictionary	луғат	[luʁat]
teach-yourself book	худомӯз	[χudomœz]
phrasebook	сӯхбатнома	[sœhbatnoma]
cassette, tape	кассета	[kasseta]
videotape	видеокассета	[videokasseta]
CD, compact disc	CD, диски компактӣ	[ɔɛ], [diski kompakti:]
DVD	DVD-диск	[ɛøɛ-disk]
alphabet	алифбо	[alifbo]
to spell (vt)	харфакӣ гап задан	[harfaki: gap zadan]
pronunciation	талаффуз	[talaffuz]
accent	зада, аксент	[zada], [aksent]
with an accent	бо аксент	[bo aksent]
without an accent	бе аксент	[be aksent]
word	калима	[kalima]
meaning	маънӣ, маъно	[ma'ni:], [ma'no]
course (e.g., a French ~)	курсхо, дарсхо	[kursho], [darsho]
to sign up	дохил шудан	[doχil ʃudan]
teacher	муаллим	[muallim]
translation (process)	тарчума	[tardʒuma]
translation (text, etc.)	тарчума	[tardʒuma]
translator	тарчумон	[tardʒumon]
interpreter	тарчумон	[tardʒumon]
polyglot	забондон	[zabondon]
memory	хофиза	[hofiza]

MEALS. RESTAURANT

48. Table setting

spoon	қошуқ	[qoʃuq]
knife	корд	[kord]
fork	чангча, чангол	[tʃangtʃa], [tʃangol]
cup (e.g., coffee ~)	косача	[kosatʃa]
plate (dinner ~)	тақсимча	[taqsimtʃa]
saucer	тақсимй, тақсимича	[taqsimi:], [taqsimitʃa]
napkin (on table)	салфетка	[salfetka]
toothpick	дандонковак	[dandonkovak]

49. Restaurant

restaurant	тарабхона	[tarabχona]
coffee house	қаҳвахона	[qahvaχona]
pub, bar	бар	[bar]
tearoom	чойхона	[tʃojχona]
waiter	пешхизмат	[peʃχizmat]
waitress	пешхизмат	[peʃχizmat]
bartender	бармен	[barmen]
menu	меню	[menju]
wine list	рӯйхати шаробҳо	[rœjχati ʃarobho]
to book a table	банд кардани миз	[band kardani miz]
course, dish	таом	[taom]
to order (meal)	супориш додан	[suporiʃ dodan]
to make an order	фармоиш додан	[farmoiʃ dodan]
aperitif	аперитив	[aperitiv]
appetizer	хӯриш, газак	[χœriʃ], [gazak]
dessert	десерт	[desert]
check	ҳисоб	[hisob]
to pay the check	пардохт кардан	[pardoχt kardan]
to give change	бақия додан	[baqija dodan]
tip	чойпулй	[tʃojpuli:]

50. Meals

food	хӯрок, таом	[xœrok], [taom]
to eat (vi, vt)	хӯрдан	[xœrdan]
breakfast	ноништа	[noniʃta]
to have breakfast	ноништа кардан	[noniʃta kardan]
lunch	хӯроки пешин	[xœroki peʃin]
to have lunch	хӯроки пешин хӯрдан	[xœroki peʃin xœrdan]
dinner	шом	[ʃom]
to have dinner	хӯроки шом хӯрдан	[xœroki ʃom xœrdan]
appetite	иштихо	[iʃtiho]
Enjoy your meal!	ош шавад!	[oʃ ʃavad]
to open (~ a bottle)	кушодан	[kuʃodan]
to spill (liquid)	резондан	[rezondan]
to spill out (vi)	рехтан	[rextan]
to boil (vi)	ҷӯшидан	[dʒœʃidan]
to boil (vt)	ҷӯшондан	[dʒœʃondan]
boiled (~ water)	ҷӯшомада	[dʒœʃomada]
to chill, cool down (vt)	хунук кардан	[xunuk kardan]
to chill (vi)	хунук шудан	[xunuk ʃudan]
taste, flavor	маза, таъм	[maza], [ta'm]
aftertaste	таъм	[ta'm]
to slim down (lose weight)	хароб шудан	[xarob ʃudan]
diet	диета	[dieta]
vitamin	витамин	[vitamin]
calorie	калория	[kalorija]
vegetarian (n)	гӯштнахӯранда	[gœʃtnaxœranda]
vegetarian (adj)	бегӯшт	[begœʃt]
fats (nutrient)	равган	[ravʁan]
proteins	сафедаҳо	[safedaho]
carbohydrates	карбогидратҳо	[karbogidratho]
slice (of lemon, ham)	тилим, порча	[tilim], [portʃa]
piece (of cake, pie)	порча	[portʃa]
crumb	резгӣ	[rezgi:]
(of bread, cake, etc.)		

51. Cooked dishes

course, dish	таом	[taom]
cuisine	таомҳо	[taomho]
recipe	ретсепт	[retsept]

portion	навола	[navola]
salad	салат	[salat]
soup	шӯрбо	[ʃœrbo]

clear soup (broth)	булён	[buljɔn]
sandwich (bread)	бутерброд	[buterbrod]
fried eggs	тухмбирён	[tuχmbirjɔn]

| hamburger (beefburger) | гамбургер | [gamburger] |
| beefsteak | бифштекс | [bifʃteks] |

side dish	хӯриши таом	[χœriʃi taom]
spaghetti	спагеттӣ	[spagetti:]
mashed potatoes	пюре	[pjure]
pizza	питса	[pitsa]
porridge (oatmeal, etc.)	шӯла	[ʃœla]
omelet	омлет, тухмбирён	[omlet], [tuχmbirjɔn]

boiled (e.g., ~ beef)	ҷӯшондашуда	[dʒœʃondaʃuda]
smoked (adj)	дудхӯрда	[dudχœrda]
fried (adj)	бирён	[birjɔn]
dried (adj)	хушк	[χuʃk]
frozen (adj)	яхкарда	[jaχkarda]
pickled (adj)	дар сирко хобондашуда	[dar sirko χobondaʃuda]

sweet (sugary)	ширин	[ʃirin]
salty (adj)	шӯр	[ʃœr]
cold (adj)	хунук	[χunuk]
hot (adj)	гарм	[garm]
bitter (adj)	талх	[talχ]
tasty (adj)	бомаза	[bomaza]

to cook in boiling water	пухтан, ҷӯшондан	[puχtan], [dʒœʃondan]
to cook (dinner)	пухтан	[puχtan]
to fry (vt)	бирён кардан	[birjɔn kardan]
to heat up (food)	гарм кардан	[garm kardan]

to salt (vt)	намак андохтан	[namak andoχtan]
to pepper (vt)	қаламфур андохтан	[qalamfur andoχtan]
to grate (vt)	тарошидан	[taroʃidan]
peel (n)	пӯст	[pœst]
to peel (vt)	пӯст кандан	[pœst kandan]

52. Food

meat	гӯшт	[gœʃt]
chicken	мурғ	[murʁ]
Rock Cornish hen (poussin)	чӯҷа	[tʃœdʒa]

duck	мурғобӣ	[murʁobi:]
goose	қоз, ғоз	[qoz], [ʁoz]
game	сайди шикор	[sajdi ʃikor]
turkey	мурғи марҷон	[murʁi mardʒon]

pork	гӯшти хук	[gœʃti χuk]
veal	гӯшти гӯсола	[gœʃti gœsola]
lamb	гӯшти гӯсфанд	[gœʃti gœsfand]
beef	гӯшти гов	[gœʃti gov]
rabbit	харгӯш	[χargœʃ]

sausage (bologna, pepperoni, etc.)	ҳасиб	[hasib]
vienna sausage (frankfurter)	ҳасибча	[hasibtʃa]
bacon	бекон	[bekon]
ham	ветчина	[vettʃina]
gammon	рон	[ron]

pâté	паштет	[paʃtet]
liver	ҷигар	[dʒigar]
hamburger (ground beef)	гӯшти кӯфта	[gœʃti kœfta]
tongue	забон	[zabon]

egg	тухм	[tuχm]
eggs	тухм	[tuχm]
egg white	сафедии тухм	[safedi:i tuχm]
egg yolk	зардии тухм	[zardi:i tuχm]

fish	моҳӣ	[mohi:]
seafood	маҳсулоти баҳрӣ	[mahsuloti bahri:]
crustaceans	буғумпойҳо	[buʁumpojho]
caviar	тухми моҳӣ	[tuχmi mohi:]

crab	харчанг	[χartʃang]
shrimp	креветка	[krevetka]
oyster	садафак	[sadafak]
spiny lobster	лангуст	[langust]
octopus	ҳаштпо	[haʃtpo]
squid	калмар	[kalmar]

sturgeon	гӯшти тосмоҳӣ	[gœʃti tosmohi:]
salmon	озодмоҳӣ	[ozodmohi:]
halibut	палтус	[paltus]

cod	равғанмоҳӣ	[ravʁanmohi:]
mackerel	зағӯтамоҳӣ	[zaʁœtamohi:]
tuna	самак	[samak]
eel	мормоҳӣ	[mormohi:]

| trout | гулмоҳӣ | [gulmohi:] |
| sardine | саморис | [samoris] |

| pike | шӯртан | [ʃœrtan] |
| herring | шӯрмоҳӣ | [ʃœrmohi:] |

bread	нон	[non]
cheese	панир	[panir]
sugar	шакар	[ʃakar]
salt	намак	[namak]

rice	биринҷ	[birinʤ]
pasta (macaroni)	макарон	[makaron]
noodles	угро	[ugro]

butter	равғани маска	[ravʁani maska]
vegetable oil	равғани пок	[ravʁani pok]
sunflower oil	равғани офтобпараст	[ravʁani oftobparast]
margarine	маргарин	[margarin]

| olives | зайтун | [zajtun] |
| olive oil | равғани зайтун | [ravʁani zajtun] |

milk	шир	[ʃir]
condensed milk	ширқиём	[ʃirqijɔm]
yogurt	йогурт	[jɔgurt]
sour cream	қаймок	[qajmok]
cream (of milk)	қаймоқ	[qajmoq]

| mayonnaise | майонез | [majɔnez] |
| buttercream | крем | [krem] |

cereal grains (wheat, etc.)	ярма	[jarma]
flour	орд	[ord]
canned food	консерв	[konserv]

cornflakes	бадроқи чуворимакка	[badroqi ʤuvorimakka]
honey	асал	[asal]
jam	чем	[ʤem]
chewing gum	сақич, илқ	[saqitʃ], [ilq]

53. Drinks

water	об	[ob]
drinking water	оби нӯшиданӣ	[obi nœʃidani:]
mineral water	оби минералӣ	[obi minerali:]

still (adj)	бе газ	[be gaz]
carbonated (adj)	газнок	[gaznok]
sparkling (adj)	газдор	[gazdor]
ice	ях	[jaχ]
with ice	бо ях, яхдор	[bo jaχ], [jaχdor]
non-alcoholic (adj)	беалкогол	[bealkogol]

soft drink	нӯшокии беалкогол	[nœʃoki:i bealkogol]
refreshing drink	нӯшокии хунук	[nœʃoki:i χunuk]
lemonade	лимонад	[limonad]

liquors	нӯшокиҳои спиртӣ	[nœʃokihoi spirti:]
wine	шароб, май	[ʃarob], [maj]
white wine	маи ангури сафед	[mai anguri safed]
red wine	маи арғувонӣ	[mai arʁuvoni:]

liqueur	ликёр	[likjɔr]
champagne	шампан	[ʃampan]
vermouth	вермут	[vermut]

whiskey	виски	[viski]
vodka	арақ, водка	[araq], [vodka]
gin	ҷин	[dʒin]
cognac	коняк	[konjak]
rum	ром	[rom]

coffee	қаҳва	[qahva]
black coffee	қаҳваи сиёҳ	[qahvai sijɔh]
coffee with milk	ширқаҳва	[ʃirqahva]
cappuccino	капучино	[kaputʃino]
instant coffee	қаҳваи кӯфта	[qahvai kœfta]

milk	шир	[ʃir]
cocktail	коктейл	[koktejl]
milkshake	коктейли ширӣ	[koktejli ʃiri:]

juice	шарбат	[ʃarbat]
tomato juice	шираи помидор	[ʃirai pomidor]
orange juice	афшураи афлесун	[afʃurai aflesun]
freshly squeezed juice	афшураи тоза тайёршуда	[afʃurai toza tajjɔrʃuda]

beer	пиво	[pivo]
light beer	оби ҷави шафоф	[obi dʒavi ʃafof]
dark beer	оби ҷави торик	[obi dʒavi torik]

tea	чой	[tʃoj]
black tea	чойи сиёҳ	[tʃoji sijɔh]
green tea	чои кабуд	[tʃoi kabud]

54. Vegetables

| vegetables | сабзавот | [sabzavot] |
| greens | сабзавот | [sabzavot] |

| tomato | помидор | [pomidor] |
| cucumber | бодиринг | [bodiring] |

carrot	сабзӣ	[sabzi:]
potato	картошка	[kartoʃka]
onion	пиёз	[pijɔz]
garlic	сир	[sir]

cabbage	карам	[karam]
cauliflower	гулкарам	[gulkaram]
Brussels sprouts	карами брусселӣ	[karami brusseli:]
broccoli	карами брокколӣ	[karami brokkoli:]

beetroot	лаблабу	[lablabu]
eggplant	бодинҷон	[bodindʒon]
zucchini	таррак	[tarrak]
pumpkin	каду	[kadu]
turnip	шалғам	[ʃalɓam]

parsley	чаъфарӣ	[dʒa'fari:]
dill	шибит	[ʃibit]
lettuce	коху	[kohu]
celery	карафс	[karafs]
asparagus	морчӯба	[mortʃœba]
spinach	испаноқ	[ispanoq]

pea	нахӯд	[naχœd]
beans	лӯбиё	[lœbijɔ]
corn (maize)	ҷуворимакка	[dʒuvorimakka]
kidney bean	лӯбиё	[lœbijɔ]

bell pepper	қаламфур	[qalamfur]
radish	шалғамча	[ʃalɓamtʃa]
artichoke	анганор	[anganor]

55. Fruits. Nuts

fruit	мева	[meva]
apple	себ	[seb]
pear	мурӯд, нок	[murœd], [nok]
lemon	лиму	[limu]
orange	афлесун, пӯртахол	[aflesun], [pœrtaχol]
strawberry (garden ~)	қулфинай	[qulfinaj]

mandarin	норанг	[norang]
plum	олу	[olu]
peach	шафтолу	[ʃaftolu]
apricot	дарахти зардолу	[daraχti zardolu]
raspberry	тамашк	[tamaʃk]
pineapple	ананас	[ananas]

| banana | банан | [banan] |
| watermelon | тарбуз | [tarbuz] |

grape	ангур	[angur]
sour cherry	олуболу	[olubolu]
sweet cherry	гелос	[gelos]

grapefruit	норинҷ	[norindʒ]
avocado	авокадо	[avokado]
papaya	папайя	[papajja]
mango	анбаҳ	[anbah]
pomegranate	анор	[anor]

redcurrant	коти сурх	[koti surχ]
blackcurrant	қоти сиёҳ	[qoti sijɔh]
gooseberry	бектошӣ	[bektoʃi:]
bilberry	черника	[tʃernika]
blackberry	марминҷон	[marmindʒon]

raisin	мавиз	[maviz]
fig	анҷир	[andʒir]
date	хурмо	[χurmo]

peanut	финдуки заминӣ	[finduki zamini:]
almond	бодом	[bodom]
walnut	чормағз	[tʃormaʁz]
hazelnut	финдиқ	[findiq]
coconut	норгил	[norgil]
pistachios	писта	[pista]

56. Bread. Candy

bakers' confectionery (pastry)	маҳсулоти қанноди	[mahsuloti qannodi]
bread	нон	[non]
cookies	кулчақанд	[kultʃaqand]

chocolate (n)	шоколад	[ʃokolad]
chocolate (as adj)	… и шоколад, шоколадӣ	[i ʃokolad], [ʃokoladi:]
candy (wrapped)	конфет	[konfet]

cake (e.g., cupcake)	пирожни	[piroʒni]
cake (e.g., birthday ~)	торт	[tort]

pie (e.g., apple ~)	пирог	[pirog]
filling (for cake, pie)	пур кардани, андохтани	[pur kardani], [andoχtani]

jam (whole fruit jam)	мураббо	[murabbo]
marmalade	мармалод	[marmalod]
waffles	вафлӣ	[vafli:]
ice-cream	яхмос	[jaχmos]
pudding	пудинг	[puding]

57. Spices

salt	намак	[namak]
salty (adj)	шӯр	[ʃœr]
to salt (vt)	намак андохтан	[namak andoχtan]
black pepper	мурчи сиёҳ	[murtʃi sijɔh]
red pepper (milled ~)	мурчи сурх	[murtʃi surχ]
mustard	хардал	[χardal]
horseradish	қаҳзак	[qahzak]
condiment	хӯриш	[χœriʃ]
spice	дорувор	[doruvor]
sauce	қайла	[qajla]
vinegar	сирко	[sirko]
anise	тухми бодиён	[tuχmi bodijɔn]
basil	нозбӯй, райҳон	[nozbœj], [rajhon]
cloves	қаланфури гардан	[qalanfuri gardan]
ginger	занҷабил	[zandʒabil]
coriander	кашнич	[kaʃnidʒ]
cinnamon	дорчин, долчин	[dortʃin], [doltʃin]
sesame	кунҷид	[kundʒid]
bay leaf	барги ғор	[bargi ʁor]
paprika	қаламфур	[qalamfur]
caraway	зира	[zira]
saffron	заъфарон	[za'faron]

PERSONAL INFORMATION. FAMILY

58. Personal information. Forms

name (first name)	ном	[nom]
surname (last name)	фамилия	[familija]
date of birth	рӯзи таваллуд	[rœzi tavallud]
place of birth	ҷойи таваллуд	[dʒoji tavallud]
nationality	миллият	[millijat]
place of residence	ҷои истиқомат	[dʒoi istiqomat]
country	кишвар	[kiʃvar]
profession (occupation)	касб	[kasb]
gender, sex	ҷинс	[dʒins]
height	қад	[qad]
weight	вазн	[vazn]

59. Family members. Relatives

mother	модар	[modar]
father	падар	[padar]
son	писар	[pisar]
daughter	духтар	[duχtar]
younger daughter	духтари хурдӣ	[duχtari χurdi:]
younger son	писари хурдӣ	[pisari χurdi:]
eldest daughter	духтари калонӣ	[duχtari kaloni:]
eldest son	писари калонӣ	[pisari kaloni:]
brother	бародар	[barodar]
elder brother	ака	[aka]
younger brother	додар	[dodar]
sister	хоҳар	[χohar]
elder sister	апа	[apa]
younger sister	хоҳари хурд	[χohari χurd]
cousin (masc.)	амакписар (ама-, таго-, хола-)	[amakpisar] ([ama], [taʁo], [χola])
cousin (fem.)	амакдухтар (ама-, таго-, хола-)	[amakduχtar] ([ama], [taʁo], [χola])
mom, mommy	модар, оча	[modar], [otʃa]
dad, daddy	дада	[dada]

parents	волидайн	[volidajn]
child	кӯдак	[kœdak]
children	бачагон, кӯдакон	[batʃagon], [kœdakon]

grandmother	модаркалон, онакалон	[modarkalon], [onakalon]
grandfather	бобо	[bobo]
grandson	набера	[nabera]
granddaughter	набера	[nabera]
grandchildren	набераҳо	[naberaho]

uncle	таѓо, амак	[taʁo], [amak]
aunt	хола, амма	[χola], [amma]
nephew	ҷиян	[dʒijan]
niece	ҷиян	[dʒijan]

mother-in-law (wife's mother)	модарарӯс	[modararœs]
father-in-law (husband's father)	падаршӯй	[padarʃœj]
son-in-law (daughter's husband)	почо, язна	[potʃo], [jazna]
stepmother	модарандар	[modarandar]
stepfather	падарандар	[padarandar]

infant	бачаи ширмак	[batʃai ʃirmak]
baby (infant)	кӯдаки ширмак	[kœdaki ʃirmak]
little boy, kid	писарча, кӯдак	[pisartʃa], [kœdak]

wife	зан	[zan]
husband	шавҳар, шӯй	[ʃavhar], [ʃœj]
spouse (husband)	завҷ	[zavdʒ]
spouse (wife)	завҷа	[zavdʒa]

married (masc.)	зандор	[zandor]
married (fem.)	шавҳардор	[ʃavhardor]
single (unmarried)	безан	[bezan]
bachelor	безан	[bezan]
divorced (masc.)	ҷудошудагӣ	[dʒudoʃudagi:]
widow	бева, бевазан	[beva], [bevazan]
widower	бева, занмурда	[beva], [zanmurda]

| relative | хеш | [χeʃ] |
| close relative | хеши наздик | [χeʃi nazdik] |

| distant relative | хеши дур | [χeʃi dur] |
| relatives | хешу табор | [χeʃu tabor] |

orphan (boy)	ятимбача	[jatimbatʃa]
orphan (girl)	ятимдухтар	[jatimduχtar]
guardian (of a minor)	васӣ	[vasi:]
to adopt (a boy)	писар хондан	[pisar χondan]
to adopt (a girl)	духтархонд кардан	[duχtarχond kardan]

60. Friends. Coworkers

friend (masc.)	дӯст, чӯра	[dœst], [dʒœra]
friend (fem.)	дугона	[dugona]
friendship	дӯстӣ, чӯрагӣ	[dœsti:], [dʒœragi:]
to be friends	дӯстӣ кардан	[dœsti: kardan]
buddy (masc.)	дуст, рафик	[dust], [rafik]
buddy (fem.)	шинос	[ʃinos]
partner	шарик	[ʃarik]
chief (boss)	сардор	[sardor]
superior (n)	сардор	[sardor]
owner, proprietor	соҳиб	[sohib]
subordinate (n)	зердаст	[zerdast]
colleague	ҳамкор	[hamkor]
acquaintance (person)	шинос, ошно	[ʃinos], [oʃno]
fellow traveler	ҳамроҳ	[hamroh]
classmate	ҳамсинф	[hamsinf]
neighbor (masc.)	ҳамсоя	[hamsoja]
neighbor (fem.)	ҳамсоязан	[hamsojazan]
neighbors	ҳамсояҳо	[hamsojaho]

HUMAN BODY. MEDICINE

61. Head

head	сар	[sar]
face	рӯй	[rœj]
nose	бинӣ	[bini:]
mouth	даҳон	[dahon]
eye	чашм, дида	[tʃaʃm], [dida]
eyes	чашмон	[tʃaʃmon]
pupil	гавҳараки чашм	[gavharaki tʃaʃm]
eyebrow	абрӯ, қош	[abrœ], [qoʃ]
eyelash	мижа	[miʒa]
eyelid	пилкҳои чашм	[pilkhoi tʃaʃm]
tongue	забон	[zabon]
tooth	дандон	[dandon]
lips	лабҳо	[labho]
cheekbones	устухони рухсора	[ustuχoni ruχsora]
gum	зираи дандон	[zirai dandon]
palate	ком	[kom]
nostrils	сурохии бинӣ	[suroχi:i bini:]
chin	манаҳ	[manah]
jaw	ҷоғ	[dʒoʁ]
cheek	рухсор	[ruχsor]
forehead	пешона	[peʃona]
temple	чакка	[tʃakka]
ear	гӯш	[gœʃ]
back of the head	пушти сар	[puʃti sar]
neck	гардан	[gardan]
throat	гулӯ	[gulœ]
hair	мӯйи сар	[mœji sar]
hairstyle	ороиши мӯйсар	[oroiʃi mœjsar]
haircut	ороиши мӯйсар	[oroiʃi mœjsar]
wig	мӯи ориятӣ	[mœi orijati:]
mustache	муйлаб, бурут	[mujlab], [burut]
beard	риш	[riʃ]
to have (a beard, etc.)	мондан, доштан	[mondan], [doʃtan]
braid	кокул	[kokul]
sideburns	риши бари рӯй	[riʃi bari rœj]
red-haired (adj)	сурхмуй	[surχmuj]

gray (hair)	сафед	[safed]
bald (adj)	одамсар	[odamsar]
bald patch	тосии сар	[tosi:i sar]
ponytail	думча	[dumt͡ʃa]
bangs	пича	[pit͡ʃa]

62. Human body

hand	панҷаи даст	[pand͡ʒai dast]
arm	даст	[dast]
finger	ангушт	[anguʃt]
toe	чилик, ангушт	[t͡ʃilik], [anguʃt]
thumb	нарангушт	[naranguʃt]
little finger	ангушти хурд	[anguʃti χurd]
nail	нохун	[noχun]
fist	кулак, мушт	[kulak], [muʃt]
palm	каф	[kaf]
wrist	банди даст	[bandi dast]
forearm	бозу	[bozu]
elbow	оринҷ	[orind͡ʒ]
shoulder	китф	[kitf]
leg	по	[po]
foot	панҷаи пой	[pand͡ʒai poj]
knee	зону	[zonu]
calf (part of leg)	соқи по	[soqi po]
hip	миён	[mijɔn]
heel	пошна	[poʃna]
body	бадан	[badan]
stomach	шикам	[ʃikam]
chest	сина	[sina]
breast	сина, пистон	[sina], [piston]
flank	паҳлу	[pahlu]
back	пушт	[puʃt]
lower back	камаргоҳ	[kamargoh]
waist	миён	[mijɔn]
navel (belly button)	ноф	[nof]
buttocks	сурин	[surin]
bottom	сурин	[surin]
beauty mark	хол	[χol]
birthmark	хол	[χol]
(café au lait spot)		
tattoo	вашм	[vaʃm]
scar	доғи захм	[doʁi zaχm]

63. Diseases

sickness	касалӣ, беморӣ	[kasali:], [bemori:]
to be sick	бемор будан	[bemor budan]
health	тандурустӣ, саломатӣ	[tandurusti:], [salomati:]
runny nose (coryza)	зуком	[zukom]
tonsillitis	дарди гулӯ	[dardi gulœ]
cold (illness)	шамол хӯрдани	[ʃamol χœrdani]
to catch a cold	шамол хӯрдан	[ʃamol χœrdan]
bronchitis	бронхит	[bronχit]
pneumonia	варами шуш	[varami ʃuʃ]
flu, influenza	грипп	[gripp]
nearsighted (adj)	наздикбин	[nazdikbin]
farsighted (adj)	дурбин	[durbin]
strabismus (crossed eyes)	олусӣ	[olusi:]
cross-eyed (adj)	олус	[olus]
cataract	катаракта	[katarakta]
glaucoma	глаукома	[glaukoma]
stroke	сактаи майна	[saktai majna]
heart attack	инфаркт, сактаи дил	[infarkt], [saktai dil]
myocardial infarction	инфаркти миокард	[infarkti miokard]
paralysis	фалач	[faladʒ]
to paralyze (vt)	фалач шудан	[faladʒ ʃudan]
allergy	аллергия	[allergija]
asthma	астма, зиққи нафас	[astma], [ziqqi nafas]
diabetes	диабет	[diabet]
toothache	дарди дандон	[dardi dandon]
caries	кариес	[karies]
diarrhea	шикамрав	[ʃikamrav]
constipation	қабзият	[qabzijat]
stomach upset	вайроншавии меъда	[vajronʃavi:i me'da]
food poisoning	захролудшавӣ	[zahroludʃavi:]
to get food poisoning	захролуд шудан	[zahrolud ʃudan]
arthritis	артрит	[artrit]
rickets	рахит, чиллаашӯр	[raχit], [tʃillaaʃœr]
rheumatism	тарбод	[tarbod]
atherosclerosis	атеросклероз	[ateroskleroz]
gastritis	гастрит	[gastrit]
appendicitis	варами кӯррӯда	[varami kœrrœda]
cholecystitis	холетсистит	[χoletsistit]
ulcer	захм	[zaχm]
measles	сурхча, сурхак	[surχtʃa], [surχak]

rubella (German measles)	сурхакон	[surχakon]
jaundice	зардча, заъфарма	[zardʧa], [za'farma]
hepatitis	гепатит, қубод	[gepatit], [qubod]

schizophrenia	маҷзубият	[madʒzubijat]
rabies (hydrophobia)	ҳорӣ	[hori:]
neurosis	невроз, чунун	[nevroz], [tʃunun]
concussion	зарб хӯрдани майна	[zarb χœrdani majna]

cancer	саратон	[saraton]
sclerosis	склероз	[skleroz]
multiple sclerosis	склерози густаришёфта	[sklerozi gustariʃʃɔfta]

alcoholism	майзадагӣ	[majzadagi:]
alcoholic (n)	майзада	[majzada]
syphilis	оташак	[otaʃak]
AIDS	СПИД	[spid]

tumor	варам	[varam]
malignant (adj)	ганда	[ganda]
benign (adj)	безарар	[bezarar]

fever	табларза, варача	[tablarza], [varadʒa]
malaria	варача	[varadʒa]
gangrene	гангрена	[gangrena]
seasickness	касалии баҳр	[kasali:i bahr]
epilepsy	саръ	[sar']

epidemic	эпидемия	[ɛpidemija]
typhus	арақа, домана	[araqa], [domana]
tuberculosis	сил	[sil]
cholera	вабо	[vabo]
plague (bubonic ~)	тоун	[toun]

64. Symptoms. Treatments. Part 1

symptom	аломат	[alomat]
temperature	ҳарорат, таб	[harorat], [tab]
high temperature (fever)	ҳарорати баланд	[harorati baland]
pulse	набз	[nabz]

dizziness (vertigo)	саргардӣ	[sargardi:]
hot (adj)	гарм	[garm]
shivering	ларза, варача	[larza], [varadʒa]
pale (e.g., ~ face)	рангпарида	[rangparida]

cough	сулфа	[sulfa]
to cough (vi)	сулфидан	[sulfidan]
to sneeze (vi)	атса задан	[atsa zadan]
faint	беҳушӣ	[behuʃi:]

to faint (vi)	беҳуш шудан	[behuʃ ʃudan]
bruise (hématome)	доғи кабуд, кабудӣ	[doʁi kabud], [kabudi:]
bump (lump)	ғуррӣ	[ʁurri:]
to bang (bump)	зада шудан	[zada ʃudan]
contusion (bruise)	лат	[lat]
to get a bruise	лату кӯб хӯрдан	[latu kœb χœrdan]

to limp (vi)	лангидан	[langidan]
dislocation	баромадан	[baromadan]
to dislocate (vt)	баровардан	[barovardan]
fracture	шикасти устухон	[ʃikasti ustuχon]
to have a fracture	устухон шикастан	[ustuχon ʃikastan]

cut (e.g., paper ~)	буриш	[buriʃ]
to cut oneself	буридан	[buridan]
bleeding	хунравӣ	[χunravi:]

| burn (injury) | сӯхта | [sœχta] |
| to get burned | сӯзондан | [sœzondan] |

to prick (vt)	халондан	[χalondan]
to prick oneself	халидан	[χalidan]
to injure (vt)	осеб дидан	[oseb didan]
injury	захм	[zaχm]
wound	захм, реш	[zaχm], [reʃ]
trauma	захм	[zaχm]

to be delirious	алой гуфтан	[aloi: guftan]
to stutter (vi)	тутила шудан	[tutila ʃudan]
sunstroke	офтобзанӣ	[oftobzani:]

65. Symptoms. Treatments. Part 2

| pain, ache | дард | [dard] |
| splinter (in foot, etc.) | хор, зиреба | [χor], [zireba] |

sweat (perspiration)	арақ	[araq]
to sweat (perspire)	арақ кардан	[araq kardan]
vomiting	қайкунӣ	[qajkuni:]
convulsions	рагкашӣ	[ragkaʃi:]

pregnant (adj)	ҳомила	[homila]
to be born	таваллуд шудан	[tavallud ʃudan]
delivery, labor	зоиш	[zoiʃ]
to deliver (~ a baby)	зоидан	[zoidan]
abortion	аборт, бачапартой	[abort], [batʃapartoi:]

in-breath (inhalation)	нафасгирӣ	[nafasgiri:]
out-breath (exhalation)	нафасбарорӣ	[nafasbarori:]
to exhale (breathe out)	нафас баровардаи	[nafas barovardai]

to inhale (vi)	нафас кашидан	[nafas kaʃidan]
disabled person	инвалид	[invalid]
cripple	маъюб	[maʼjub]
drug addict	нашъаманд	[naʃʼamand]

deaf (adj)	кар, гӯшкар	[kar], [gœʃkar]
mute (adj)	гунг	[gung]
deaf mute (adj)	кару гунг	[karu gung]

mad, insane (adj)	девона	[devona]
madman (demented person)	девона	[devona]
madwoman	девона	[devona]
to go insane	аз ақл бегона шудан	[az aql begona ʃudan]

gene	ген	[gen]
immunity	сироятнопазирӣ	[sirojatnopaziri:]
hereditary (adj)	меросӣ, ирсӣ	[merosi:], [irsi:]
congenital (adj)	модарзод	[modarzod]

virus	вирус	[virus]
microbe	микроб	[mikrob]
bacterium	бактерия	[bakterija]
infection	сироят	[sirojat]

66. Symptoms. Treatments. Part 3

| hospital | касалхона | [kasalχona] |
| patient | бемор | [bemor] |

diagnosis	ташхиси касалӣ	[taʃχisi kasali:]
cure	муолича	[muoliʤa]
medical treatment	табобат	[tabobat]
to get treatment	табобат гирифтан	[tabobat giriftan]
to treat (~ a patient)	табобат кардан	[tabobat kardan]
to nurse (look after)	нигоҳубин кардан	[nigohubin kardan]
care (nursing ~)	нигоҳубин	[nigohubin]

operation, surgery	ҷарроҳи	[ʤarrohi]
to bandage (head, limb)	бо бандина бастан	[bo bandina bastan]
bandaging	ҷароҳатбандӣ	[ʤarohatbandi:]

vaccination	доругузаронӣ	[doruguzaroni:]
to vaccinate (vt)	эмгузаронӣ кардан	[ɛmguzaroni: kardan]
injection, shot	сӯзанзанӣ	[sœzanzani:]
to give an injection	сӯзандору кардан	[sœzandoru kardan]

attack	хуруҷ	[χuruʤ]
amputation	ампутатсия	[amputatsija]
to amputate (vt)	ампутатсия кардан	[amputatsija kardan]

coma	кома, игмо	[koma], [igmo]
to be in a coma	дар кома будан	[dar koma budan]
intensive care	шӯъбаи эҳё	[ʃœ'bai ɛhjɔ]

to recover (~ from flu)	сиҳат шудан	[sihat ʃudan]
condition (patient's ~)	аҳвол	[ahvol]
consciousness	ҳуш	[huʃ]
memory (faculty)	ҳофиза	[hofiza]

to pull out (tooth)	кандан	[kandan]
filling	пломба	[plomba]
to fill (a tooth)	пломба занондан	[plomba zanondan]

| hypnosis | гипноз | [gipnoz] |
| to hypnotize (vt) | гипноз кардан | [gipnoz kardan] |

67. Medicine. Drugs. Accessories

medicine, drug	дору	[doru]
remedy	дору	[doru]
to prescribe (vt)	таъйин кардан	[ta'jin kardan]
prescription	нусхаи даво	[nusχai davo]

tablet, pill	ҳаб	[hab]
ointment	марҳам	[marham]
ampule	ампул	[ampul]
mixture	доруи обакӣ	[dorui obaki:]
syrup	сироп	[sirop]
pill	ҳаб	[hab]
powder	хока	[χoka]

gauze bandage	дока	[doka]
cotton wool	пахта	[paχta]
iodine	йод	[jɔd]

Band-Aid	лейкопластир	[lejkoplastir]
eyedropper	қатрачакон	[qatratʃakon]
thermometer	ҳароратсанҷ	[haroratsandʒ]
syringe	обдуздак	[obduzdak]

| wheelchair | аробачаи маъюбӣ | [arobatʃai ma'jubi:] |
| crutches | бағаласо | [baʁalaso] |

painkiller	доруи дард	[dorui dard]
laxative	мусҳил	[mushil]
spirits (ethanol)	спирт	[spirt]
medicinal herbs	растаниҳои доругӣ	[rastanihoi dorugi:]
herbal (~ tea)	… и алаф	[i alaf]

APARTMENT

68. Apartment

apartment	манзил	[manzil]
room	хона, ӯтоқ	[χona], [œtoq]
bedroom	хонаи хоб	[χonai χob]
dining room	хонаи хӯрокхӯрӣ	[χonai χœrokχœri:]
living room	меҳмонхона	[mehmonχona]
study (home office)	уток	[utoq]
entry room	мадхал, даҳлез	[madχal], [dahlez]
bathroom (room with a bath or shower)	ваннахона	[vannaχona]
half bath	ҳоҷатхона	[hoʤatχona]
ceiling	шифт	[ʃift]
floor	фарш	[farʃ]
corner	кунҷ	[kunʤ]

69. Furniture. Interior

furniture	мебел	[mebel]
table	миз	[miz]
chair	курсӣ	[kursi:]
bed	кат	[kat]
couch, sofa	диван	[divan]
armchair	курсӣ	[kursi:]
bookcase	чевони китобмонӣ	[ʤevoni kitobmoni:]
shelf	раф, рафча	[raf], [raftʃa]
wardrobe	чевони либос	[ʤevoni libos]
coat rack (wall-mounted ~)	либосовезак	[libosovezak]
coat stand	либосовезак	[libosovezak]
bureau, dresser	чевон	[ʤevon]
coffee table	мизи қаҳва	[mizi qahva]
mirror	оина	[oina]
carpet	гилем, қолин	[gilem], [qolin]
rug, small carpet	гилемча	[gilemtʃa]
fireplace	оташдон	[otaʃdon]
candle	шамъ	[ʃam']

candlestick	шамъдон	[ʃamʼdon]
drapes	парда	[parda]
wallpaper	зардеворӣ	[zardevori:]
blinds (jalousie)	жалюзи	[ʒaljuzi]

table lamp	чароғи мизӣ	[tʃaroʁi mizi:]
wall lamp (sconce)	чароғак	[tʃaroʁak]
floor lamp	торшер	[torʃer]
chandelier	қандил	[qandil]

leg (of chair, table)	поя	[poja]
armrest	оринҷмонаки курсӣ	[orindʒmonaki kursi:]
back (backrest)	пуштаки курсӣ	[puʃtaki kursi:]
drawer	ғаладон	[ʁaladon]

70. Bedding

bedclothes	чилдҳои болишту бистар	[dʒildhoi boliʃtu bistar]
pillow	болишт	[boliʃt]
pillowcase	чилди болишт	[dʒildi boliʃt]
duvet, comforter	кӯрпа	[kœrpa]
sheet	ҷойпӯш	[dʒojpœʃ]
bedspread	болопӯш	[bolopœʃ]

71. Kitchen

kitchen	ошхона	[oʃχona]
gas	газ	[gaz]
gas stove (range)	плитаи газ	[plitai gaz]
electric stove	плитаи электрикӣ	[plitai ɛlektriki:]
microwave oven	микроволновка	[mikrovolnovka]

refrigerator	яхдон	[jaχdon]
freezer	яхдон	[jaχdon]
dishwasher	мошини зарфшӯй	[moʃini zarfʃœj]

meat grinder	мошини гӯштҷӯбӣ	[moʃini gœʃtkœbi:]
juicer	шарбатафшурак	[ʃarbatafʃurak]
toaster	тостер	[toster]
mixer	миксер	[mikser]

coffee machine	қаҳваҷӯшонак	[qahvadʒœʃonak]
coffee pot	зарфи қаҳваҷӯшонӣ	[zarfi qahvadʒœʃoni:]
coffee grinder	дастоси қаҳва	[dastosi qahva]

| kettle | чойник | [tʃojnik] |
| teapot | чойник | [tʃojnik] |

lid	сарпӯш	[sarpœʃ]
tea strainer	ғалберча	[ʁalbertʃa]
spoon	қошуқ	[qoʃuq]
teaspoon	чойкошук	[tʃojkoʃuk]
soup spoon	қошуқи ошхӯрӣ	[qoʃuqi oʃχœri:]
fork	чангча, чангол	[tʃangtʃa], [tʃangol]
knife	корд	[kord]
tableware (dishes)	табақ	[tabaq]
plate (dinner ~)	тақсимча	[taqsimtʃa]
saucer	тақсимӣ, тақсимича	[taqsimi:], [taqsimitʃa]
shot glass	рюмка	[rjumka]
glass (tumbler)	стакан	[stakan]
cup	косача	[kosatʃa]
sugar bowl	шакардон	[ʃakardon]
salt shaker	намакдон	[namakdon]
pepper shaker	қаламфурдон	[qalamfurdon]
butter dish	равғандон	[ravʁandon]
stock pot (soup pot)	дегча	[degtʃa]
frying pan (skillet)	тоба	[toba]
ladle	кафлез, обгардон, сархумӣ	[kaflez], [obgardon], [sarχumi:]
tray (serving ~)	лаълӣ	[la'li:]
bottle	шиша, сурохӣ	[ʃiʃa], [surohi:]
jar (glass)	банкаи шишагӣ	[bankai ʃiʃagi:]
can	банкаи тунукагӣ	[bankai tunukagi:]
bottle opener	саркушояк	[sarkuʃojak]
can opener	саркушояк	[sarkuʃojak]
corkscrew	пӯккашак	[pœkkaʃak]
filter	филтр	[filtr]
to filter (vt)	полоидан	[poloidan]
trash, garbage (food waste, etc.)	ахлот	[aχlot]
trash can (kitchen ~)	сатили ахлот	[satili aχlot]

72. Bathroom

bathroom	ваннахона	[vannaχona]
water	об	[ob]
faucet	чуммак, мил	[dʒummak], [mil]
hot water	оби гарм	[obi garm]
cold water	оби сард	[obi sard]
toothpaste	хамираи дандон	[χamirai dandon]

| to brush one's teeth | дандон шустан | [dandon ʃustan] |
| toothbrush | чӯткаи дандоншӯй | [tʃœtkai dandonʃœi:] |

to shave (vi)	риш гирифтан	[riʃ giriftan]
shaving foam	кафки ришгирй	[kafki riʃgiri:]
razor	ришгирак	[riʃgirak]

to wash (one's hands, etc.)	шустан	[ʃustan]
to take a bath	шустушӯ кардан	[ʃustuʃœ kardan]
to take a shower	ба душ даромадан	[ba duʃ daromadan]

bathtub	ванна	[vanna]
toilet (toilet bowl)	нишастгоҳи халочо	[niʃastgohi χalodʒo]
sink (washbasin)	дастшӯяк	[dastʃœjak]

| soap | собун | [sobun] |
| soap dish | собундон | [sobundon] |

sponge	исфанч	[isfandʒ]
shampoo	шампун	[ʃampun]
towel	сачоқ	[satʃoq]
bathrobe	халат	[χalat]

laundry (process)	чомашӯй	[dʒomaʃœi:]
washing machine	мошини чомашӯй	[moʃini dʒomaʃœi:]
to do the laundry	чомашӯй кардан	[dʒomaʃœi: kardan]
laundry detergent	хокаи чомашӯй	[χokai dʒomaʃœi:]

73. Household appliances

TV set	телевизор	[televizor]
tape recorder	магнитафон	[magnitafon]
VCR (video recorder)	видеомагнитафон	[videomagnitafon]
radio	радио	[radio]
player (CD, MP3, etc.)	плеер	[pleer]

video projector	видеопроектор	[videoproektor]
home movie theater	кинотеатри хонагй	[kinoteatri χonagi:]
DVD player	DVD-монак	[ɛøɛ-monak]
amplifier	қувватафзо	[quvvatafzo]
video game console	плейстейшн	[plejstejʃn]

video camera	видеокамера	[videokamera]
camera (photo)	фотоаппарат	[fotoapparat]
digital camera	суратгираки рақамй	[suratgiraki raqami:]

vacuum cleaner	чангкашак	[tʃangkaʃak]
iron (e.g., steam ~)	дарзмол	[darzmol]
ironing board	тахтаи дарзмолкунй	[taχtai darzmolkuni:]
telephone	телефон	[telefon]

cell phone	телефони мобилй	[telefoni mobili:]
typewriter	мошинаи хатнависй	[moʃinai χatnavisi:]
sewing machine	мошинаи чокдӯзй	[moʃinai ʧokdœzi:]

microphone	микрофон	[mikrofon]
headphones	гӯшак, гӯшпӯшак	[ɡœʃak], [ɡœʃpœʃak]
remote control (TV)	пулт	[pult]

CD, compact disc	компакт-диск	[kompakt-disk]
cassette, tape	кассета	[kasseta]
vinyl record	пластинка	[plastinka]

THE EARTH. WEATHER

74. Outer space

space	кайҳон	[kajhon]
space (as adj)	... и кайҳон	[i kajhon]
outer space	фазои кайҳон	[fazoi kajhon]
world	ҷаҳон	[dʒahon]
universe	коинот	[koinot]
galaxy	галактика	[galaktika]
star	ситора	[sitora]
constellation	бурҷ	[burdʒ]
planet	сайёра	[sajjɔra]
satellite	радиф	[radif]
meteorite	метеорит, шиҳобпора	[meteorit], [ʃihobpora]
comet	ситораи думдор	[sitorai dumdor]
asteroid	астероид	[asteroid]
orbit	мадор	[mador]
to revolve (~ around the Earth)	давр задан	[davr zadan]
atmosphere	атмосфера	[atmosfera]
the Sun	Офтоб	[oftob]
solar system	манзумаи шамсӣ	[manzumai ʃamsi:]
solar eclipse	гирифтани офтоб	[giriftani oftob]
the Earth	Замин	[zamin]
the Moon	Моҳ	[moh]
Mars	Миррих	[mirriχ]
Venus	Зӯҳра, Ноҳид	[zœhra], [nohid]
Jupiter	Муштарӣ	[muʃtari:]
Saturn	Кайвон	[kajvon]
Mercury	Уторид	[utorid]
Uranus	Уран	[uran]
Neptune	Нептун	[neptun]
Pluto	Плутон	[pluton]
Milky Way	Роҳи Каҳкашон	[rohi kahkaʃon]
Great Bear (Ursa Major)	Дубби Акбар	[dubbi akbar]
North Star	Ситораи қутбӣ	[sitorai qutbi:]
Martian	миррихӣ	[mirriχi:]

extraterrestrial (n)	инопланетянхо	[inoplanetjanho]
alien	махлукӣ кайҳонӣ	[maxluqi: kajhoni:]
flying saucer	табақи парвозкунанда	[tabaqi parvozkunanda]

spaceship	киштии кайҳонӣ	[kiʃti:i kajhoni:]
space station	стантсияи мадорӣ	[stantsijai madori:]
blast-off	оғоз	[oʁoz]

engine	муҳаррик	[muharrik]
nozzle	сопло	[soplo]
fuel	сӯзишворӣ	[sœziʃvori:]

cockpit, flight deck	кабина	[kabina]
antenna	антенна	[antenna]
porthole	иллюминатор	[illjuminator]
solar panel	батареи офтобӣ	[batarei oftobi:]
spacesuit	скафандр	[skafandr]

| weightlessness | бевазнӣ | [bevazni:] |
| oxygen | оксиген | [oksigen] |

| docking (in space) | пайваст | [pajvast] |
| to dock (vi, vt) | пайваст кардан | [pajvast kardan] |

observatory	расадхона	[rasadxona]
telescope	телескоп	[teleskop]
to observe (vt)	мушоҳида кардан	[muʃohida kardan]
to explore (vt)	таҳқиқ кардан	[tahqiq kardan]

75. The Earth

the Earth	Замин	[zamin]
the globe (the Earth)	кураи замин	[kurai zamin]
planet	сайёра	[sajjora]

atmosphere	атмосфера	[atmosfera]
geography	география	[geografija]
nature	табиат	[tabiat]

globe (table ~)	глобус	[globus]
map	харита	[xarita]
atlas	атлас	[atlas]

Asia	Осиё	[osijɔ]
Africa	Африқо	[afriqo]
Australia	Австралия	[avstralija]

America	Америка	[amerika]
North America	Америкаи Шимолӣ	[amerikai ʃimoli:]
South America	Америкаи Ҷанубӣ	[amerikai dʒanubi:]

| Antarctica | Антарктида | [antarktida] |
| the Arctic | Арктика | [arktika] |

76. Cardinal directions

north	шимол	[ʃimol]
to the north	ба шимол	[ba ʃimol]
in the north	дар шимол	[dar ʃimol]
northern (adj)	шимолӣ, ... и шимол	[ʃimoli:], [i ʃimol]

south	ҷануб	[dʒanub]
to the south	ба ҷануб	[ba dʒanub]
in the south	дар ҷануб	[dar dʒanub]
southern (adj)	ҷанубӣ, ... и ҷануб	[dʒanubi:], [i dʒanub]

west	ғарб	[ʁarb]
to the west	ба ғарб	[ba ʁarb]
in the west	дар ғарб	[dar ʁarb]
western (adj)	ғарбӣ, ... и ғарб	[ʁarbi:], [i ʁarb]

east	шарқ	[ʃarq]
to the east	ба шарқ	[ba ʃarq]
in the east	дар шарқ	[dar ʃarq]
eastern (adj)	шарқӣ	[ʃarqi:]

77. Sea. Ocean

sea	баҳр	[bahr]
ocean	уқёнус	[uqjɔnus]
gulf (bay)	халиҷ	[xalidʒ]
straits	гулӯгоҳ	[gulœgoh]

| land (solid ground) | хушкӣ, замин | [xuʃki:], [zamin] |
| continent (mainland) | материк, қитъа | [materik], [qit'a] |

island	ҷазира	[dʒazira]
peninsula	нимҷазира	[nimdʒazira]
archipelago	галаҷазира	[galadʒazira]

bay, cove	халиҷ	[xalidʒ]
harbor	бандар	[bandar]
lagoon	лагуна	[laguna]
cape	димоға	[dimoʁa]

atoll	атолл	[atoll]
reef	харсанги зериобӣ	[xarsangi zeriobi:]
coral	марҷон	[mardʒon]
coral reef	обсанги марҷонӣ	[obsangi mardʒoni:]

deep (adj)	чуқур	[tʃuqur]
depth (deep water)	чуқурӣ	[tʃuquri:]
abyss	қаър	[qaʼr]
trench (e.g., Mariana ~)	чуқурӣ	[tʃuquri:]

| current (Ocean ~) | чараён | [dʒarajɔn] |
| to surround (bathe) | шустан | [ʃustan] |

| shore | соҳил, соҳили баҳр | [sohil], [sohili bahr] |
| coast | соҳил | [sohil] |

flow (flood tide)	мадд	[madd]
ebb (ebb tide)	чазр	[dʒazr]
shoal	пастоб	[pastob]
bottom (~ of the sea)	қаър	[qaʼr]

wave	мавч	[mavdʒ]
crest (~ of a wave)	теғаи мавч	[teʁai mavdʒ]
spume (sea foam)	кафк	[kafk]

storm (sea storm)	тӯфон, бӯрои	[tœfon], [bœroi]
hurricane	тундбод	[tundbod]
tsunami	сунами	[sunami]
calm (dead ~)	сукунати ҳаво	[sukunati havo]
quiet, calm (adj)	ором	[orom]

| pole | қутб | [qutb] |
| polar (adj) | қутбӣ | [qutbi:] |

latitude	арз	[arz]
longitude	тӯл	[tœl]
parallel	параллел	[parallel]
equator	хати истиво	[χati istivo]

sky	осмон	[osmon]
horizon	уфуқ	[ufuq]
air	ҳаво	[havo]

lighthouse	мино	[mino]
to dive (vi)	ғӯта задан	[ʁœta zadan]
to sink (ab. boat)	ғарқ шудан	[ʁarq ʃudan]
treasures	ганч	[gandʒ]

78. Seas' and Oceans' names

Atlantic Ocean	Уқёнуси Атлантик	[uqjɔnusi atlantik]
Indian Ocean	Уқёнуси Ҳинд	[uqjɔnusi hind]
Pacific Ocean	Уқёнуси Ором	[uqjɔnusi orom]
Arctic Ocean	Уқёнуси яхбастаи шимолӣ	[uqjɔnusi jaχbastai ʃimoli:]

Black Sea	Баҳри Сиёҳ	[bahri sijɔh]
Red Sea	Баҳри Сурх	[bahri surχ]
Yellow Sea	Баҳри Зард	[bahri zard]
White Sea	Баҳри Сафед	[bahri safed]

Caspian Sea	Баҳри Хазар	[bahri χazar]
Dead Sea	Баҳри Майит	[bahri majit]
Mediterranean Sea	Баҳри Миёназамин	[bahri mijɔnazamin]

| Aegean Sea | Баҳри Эгей | [bahri ɛgej] |
| Adriatic Sea | Баҳри Адриатика | [bahri adriatika] |

Arabian Sea	Баҳри Арави	[bahri aravi]
Sea of Japan	Баҳри Ҷопон	[bahri dʒopon]
Bering Sea	Баҳри Беринг	[bahri bering]
South China Sea	Баҳри Хитойи Ҷанубй	[bahri χitoji dʒanubi:]

Coral Sea	Баҳри Марҷон	[bahri mardʒon]
Tasman Sea	Баҳри Тасман	[bahri tasman]
Caribbean Sea	Баҳри Кариб	[bahri karib]

| Barents Sea | Баҳри Баренс | [bahri barens] |
| Kara Sea | Баҳри Кара | [bahri kara] |

North Sea	Баҳри Шимолй	[bahri ʃimoli:]
Baltic Sea	Баҳри Балтика	[bahri baltika]
Norwegian Sea	Баҳри Норвегия	[bahri norvegija]

79. Mountains

mountain	кӯҳ	[kœh]
mountain range	силсилакӯҳ	[silsilakœh]
mountain ridge	қаторкӯҳ	[qatorkœh]

summit, top	кулла	[kulla]
peak	қулла	[qulla]
foot (~ of the mountain)	доманаи кӯҳ	[domanai kœh]
slope (mountainside)	нишебй	[niʃebi:]

volcano	вулқон	[vulqon]
active volcano	вулқони амалкунанда	[vulqoni amalkunanda]
dormant volcano	вулқони хомӯшшуда	[vulqoni χomœʃʃuda]

eruption	оташфишонй	[otaʃfiʃoni:]
crater	танӯра	[tanœra]
magma	магма, тафта	[magma], [tafta]
lava	гудоза	[gudoza]
molten (~ lava)	тафта	[tafta]
canyon	оббурда, дара	[obburda], [dara]

gorge	дара	[dara]
crevice	тангно	[tangno]
abyss (chasm)	партгох	[partgoh]

pass, col	агба	[aʁba]
plateau	пуштаи кӯх	[puʃtai kœh]
cliff	шух	[ʃuχ]
hill	теппа	[teppa]

glacier	пирях	[pirjaχ]
waterfall	шаршара	[ʃarʃara]
geyser	гейзер	[gejzer]
lake	кул	[kul]

plain	хамворӣ	[hamvori:]
landscape	манзара	[manzara]
echo	акси садо	[aksi sado]

alpinist	кӯхнавард	[kœhnavard]
rock climber	шухпаймо	[ʃuχpajmo]
to conquer (in climbing)	фатх кардан	[fath kardan]
climb (an easy ~)	болобарой	[bolobaroi:]

80. Mountains names

The Alps	Кӯххои Алп	[kœhhoi alp]
Mont Blanc	Монблан	[monblan]
The Pyrenees	Кӯххои Пиреней	[kœhhoi pirenej]

The Carpathians	Кӯххои Карпат	[kœhhoi karpat]
The Ural Mountains	Кӯххои Урал	[kœhhoi ural]
The Caucasus Mountains	Кӯххои Кавказ	[kœhhoi kavkaz]
Mount Elbrus	Елбруз	[elbruz]

The Altai Mountains	Алтай	[altaj]
The Tian Shan	Тиёншон	[tijɔnʃon]
The Pamir Mountains	Кӯххои Помир	[kœhhoi pomir]
The Himalayas	Химолой	[himoloj]
Mount Everest	Эверест	[ɛverest]

| The Andes | Кӯххои Анд | [kœhhoi and] |
| Mount Kilimanjaro | Килиманчаро | [kilimandʒaro] |

81. Rivers

river	дарё	[darjɔ]
spring (natural source)	чашма	[tʃaʃma]
riverbed (river channel)	мачрои дарё	[madʒroi darjɔ]

basin (river valley)	ҳавза	[havza]
to flow into ...	рехтан ба ...	[reχtan ba]
tributary	шохоб	[ʃoχob]
bank (of river)	соҳил	[sohil]
current (stream)	ҷараён	[dʒarajɔn]
downstream (adv)	мувофиқи рафти об	[muvofiqi rafti ob]
upstream (adv)	муқобили самти об	[muqobili samti ob]
inundation	обхезӣ	[obχezi:]
flooding	обхез	[obχez]
to overflow (vi)	дамидан	[damidan]
to flood (vt)	зер кардан	[zer kardan]
shallow (shoal)	тунукоба	[tunukoba]
rapids	мавҷрез	[mavdʒrez]
dam	сарбанд	[sarband]
canal	канал	[kanal]
reservoir (artificial lake)	обанбор	[obanbor]
sluice, lock	шлюз	[ʃljuz]
water body (pond, etc.)	обанбор	[obanbor]
swamp (marshland)	ботлоқ, ботқоқ	[botloq], [botqoq]
bog, marsh	ботлоқ	[botloq]
whirlpool	гирдоб	[girdob]
stream (brook)	ҷӯй	[dʒœj]
drinking (ab. water)	нӯшиданӣ	[nœʃidani:]
fresh (~ water)	ширин	[ʃirin]
ice	ях	[jaχ]
to freeze over (ab. river, etc.)	ях бастан	[jaχ bastan]

82. Rivers' names

Seine	Сена	[sena]
Loire	Луара	[luara]
Thames	Темза	[temza]
Rhine	Рейн	[rejn]
Danube	Дунай	[dunaj]
Volga	Волга	[volga]
Don	Дон	[don]
Lena	Лена	[lena]
Yellow River	Хуанхе	[χuanχe]
Yangtze	Янсзи	[janszi]

Mekong	Меконг	[mekong]
Ganges	Ганга	[ganga]
Nile River	Нил	[nil]
Congo River	Конго	[kongo]
Okavango River	Окаванго	[okavango]
Zambezi River	Замбези	[zambezi]
Limpopo River	Лимпопо	[limpopo]
Mississippi River	Миссисипи	[missisipi]

83. Forest

forest, wood	ҷангал	[dʒangal]
forest (as adj)	ҷангалй	[dʒangali:]
thick forest	ҷангалзор	[dʒangalzor]
grove	дарахтзор	[daraχtzor]
forest clearing	чаман	[tʃaman]
thicket	буттазор	[buttazor]
scrubland	буттазор	[buttazor]
footpath (trodden path)	пайраҳа	[pajraha]
gully	оббурда	[obburda]
tree	дарахт	[daraχt]
leaf	барг	[barg]
leaves (foliage)	баргҳои дарахт	[barghoi daraχt]
fall of leaves	баргрезй	[bargrezi:]
to fall (ab. leaves)	рехтан	[reχtan]
top (of the tree)	нӯг	[nœg]
branch	шох, шохча	[ʃoχ], [ʃoχtʃa]
bough	шохи дарахг	[ʃoχi daraχg]
bud (on shrub, tree)	муғча	[muʁdʒa]
needle (of pine tree)	сӯзан	[sœzan]
pine cone	ҷалғӯза	[dʒalʁœza]
hollow (in a tree)	сӯрохи дарахт	[sœroχi daraχt]
nest	ошёна, лона	[oʃjona], [lona]
burrow (animal hole)	хона	[χona]
trunk	тана	[tana]
root	реша	[reʃa]
bark	пӯсти дарахт	[pœsti daraχt]
moss	ушна	[uʃna]
to uproot (remove trees or tree stumps)	реша кофтан	[reʃa koftan]
to chop down	зада буридан	[zada buridan]

to deforest (vt)	бурида нест кардан	[burida nest kardan]
tree stump	кундаи дарахт	[kundai daraxt]
campfire	гулхан	[gulxan]
forest fire	сӯхтор, оташ	[sœxtor], [otaʃ]
to extinguish (vt)	хомӯш кардан	[xomœʃ kardan]
forest ranger	ҷангалбон	[dʒangalbon]
protection	нигоҳбонӣ	[nigohboni:]
to protect (~ nature)	нигоҳбонӣ кардан	[nigohboni: kardan]
poacher	қӯруқшикан	[qœruqʃikan]
steel trap	қапқон, дом	[qapqon], [dom]
to gather, to pick (vt)	чидан	[tʃidan]
to lose one's way	роҳ гум кардан	[roh gum kardan]

84. Natural resources

natural resources	захираҳои табиӣ	[zaxirahoi tabi:i:]
minerals	маъданҳои фоиданок	[ma'danhoi foidanok]
deposits	кон, маъдаи	[kon], [ma'dai]
field (e.g., oilfield)	кон	[kon]
to mine (extract)	кандан	[kandan]
mining (extraction)	кандани	[kandani:]
ore	маъдан	[ma'dan]
mine (e.g., for coal)	кон	[kon]
shaft (mine ~)	чоҳ	[tʃoh]
miner	конкан	[konkan]
gas (natural ~)	газ	[gaz]
gas pipeline	қубури газ	[quburi gaz]
oil (petroleum)	нефт	[neft]
oil pipeline	қубури нефт	[quburi neft]
oil well	чоҳи нафт	[tʃohi naft]
derrick (tower)	бурҷи нафткашӣ	[burdʒi naftkaʃi:]
tanker	танкер	[tanker]
sand	рег	[reg]
limestone	оҳаксанг	[ohaksang]
gravel	сангреза, шағал	[sangreza], [ʃaʁal]
peat	торф	[torf]
clay	гил	[gil]
coal	ангишт	[angiʃt]
iron (ore)	оҳан	[ohan]
gold	зар, тилло	[zar], [tillo]
silver	нуқра	[nuqra]
nickel	никел	[nikel]

copper	мис	[mis]
zinc	рух	[ruh]
manganese	манган	[mangan]
mercury	симоб	[simob]
lead	сурб	[surb]
mineral	минерал, маъдан	[mineral], [ma'dan]
crystal	булӯр, шӯша	[bulœr], [ʃœʃa]
marble	мармар	[marmar]
uranium	уран	[uran]

85. Weather

weather	обу ҳаво	[obu havo]
weather forecast	пешгӯии ҳаво	[peʃgœi:i havo]
temperature	ҳарорат	[harorat]
thermometer	ҳароратсанҷ	[haroratsandʒ]
barometer	барометр, ҳавосанҷ	[barometr], [havosandʒ]
humid (adj)	намнок	[namnok]
humidity	намӣ, рутубат	[nami:], [rutubat]
heat (extreme ~)	гармӣ	[garmi:]
hot (torrid)	тафсон	[tafson]
it's hot	ҳаво тафсон аст	[havo tafson ast]
it's warm	ҳаво гарм аст	[havo garm ast]
warm (moderately hot)	гарм	[garm]
it's cold	ҳаво сард аст	[havo sard ast]
cold (adj)	хунук, сард	[xunuk], [sard]
sun	офтоб	[oftob]
to shine (vi)	тобидан	[tobidan]
sunny (day)	… и офтоб	[i oftob]
to come up (vi)	баромадан	[baromadan]
to set (vi)	паст шудан	[past ʃudan]
cloud	абр	[abr]
cloudy (adj)	… и абр, абрӣ	[i abr], [abri:]
rain cloud	абри сиёҳ	[abri sijoh]
somber (gloomy)	абрнок	[abrnok]
rain	борон	[boron]
it's raining	борон меборад	[boron meborad]
rainy (~ day, weather)	серборон	[serboron]
to drizzle (vi)	сим-сим боридан	[sim-sim boridan]
pouring rain	борони сахт	[boroni saxt]
downpour	борони сел	[boroni sel]

heavy (e.g., ~ rain)	сахт	[saχt]
puddle	кӯлмак	[kœlmak]
to get wet (in rain)	шилтиқ шудан	[ʃiltiq ʃudan]
fog (mist)	туман	[tuman]
foggy	... и туман	[i tuman]
snow	барф	[barf]
it's snowing	барф меборад	[barf meborad]

86. Severe weather. Natural disasters

thunderstorm	раъду барк	[ra'du bark]
lightning (~ strike)	барқ	[barq]
to flash (vi)	дурахшидан	[duraχʃidan]
thunder	тундар	[tundar]
to thunder (vi)	гулдуррос задан	[guldurros zadan]
it's thundering	раъд гулдуррос мезанад	[ra'd guldurros mezanad]
hail	жола	[ʒola]
it's hailing	жола меборад	[ʒola meborad]
to flood (vt)	зер кардан	[zer kardan]
flood, inundation	обхезӣ	[obχezi:]
earthquake	заминчунбӣ	[zamindʒunbi:]
tremor, quake	заминчунбӣ,такон	[zamindʒunbi:,takon]
epicenter	эпимарказ	[ɛpimarkaz]
eruption	оташфишонӣ	[otaʃfiʃoni:]
lava	гудоза	[gudoza]
twister	гирдбод	[girdbod]
tornado	торнадо	[tornado]
typhoon	тӯфон	[tœfon]
hurricane	тундбод	[tundbod]
storm	тӯфон, бӯрои	[tœfon], [bœroi]
tsunami	сунами	[sunami]
cyclone	сиклон	[siklon]
bad weather	ҳавои бад	[havoi bad]
fire (accident)	сӯхтор, оташ	[sœχtor], [otaʃ]
disaster	садама, фалокат	[sadama], [falokat]
meteorite	метеорит, шихобпора	[meteorit], [ʃihobpora]
avalanche	тарма	[tarma]
snowslide	тарма	[tarma]
blizzard	бӯрони барфӣ	[bœroni barfi:]

| snowstorm | бӯрон | [bœron] |

FAUNA

87. Mammals. Predators

predator	дарранда	[darranda]
tiger	бабр, паланг	[babr], [palang]
lion	шер	[ʃer]
wolf	гург	[gurg]
fox	рӯбоҳ	[rœboh]
jaguar	юзи ало	[juzi alo]
leopard	паланг	[palang]
cheetah	юз	[juz]
black panther	пантера	[pantera]
puma	пума	[puma]
snow leopard	шерпаланг	[ʃerpalang]
lynx	силовсин	[silovsin]
coyote	койот	[kojɔt]
jackal	шагол	[ʃagol]
hyena	кафтор	[kaftor]

88. Wild animals

animal	ҳайвон	[hajvon]
beast (animal)	ҳайвони ваҳшӣ	[hajvoni vahʃi:]
squirrel	санҷоб	[sandʒob]
hedgehog	хорпушт	[χorpuʃt]
hare	зарғӯш	[zargœʃ]
rabbit	харғӯш	[χargœʃ]
badger	қашқалдоқ	[qaʃqaldoq]
raccoon	енот	[enot]
hamster	миримӯшон	[mirimœʃon]
marmot	суғур	[suʁur]
mole	кӯрмуш	[kœrmuʃ]
mouse	муш	[muʃ]
rat	калламуш	[kallamuʃ]
bat	кӯршапарак	[kœrʃaparak]
ermine	қоқум	[qoqum]
sable	самур	[samur]

marten	савсор	[savsor]
weasel	росу	[rosu]
mink	вашақ	[vaʃaq]

beaver	кундуз	[kunduz]
otter	сағоби	[sagobi]

horse	асп	[asp]
moose	шоҳгавазн	[ʃohgavazn]
deer	гавазн	[gavazn]
camel	шутур, уштур	[ʃutur], [uʃtur]

bison	бизон	[bizon]
aurochs	гови ваҳшй	[govi vahʃi:]
buffalo	говмеш	[govmeʃ]

zebra	гӯрхар	[gœrχar]
antelope	антилопа, ғизол	[antilopa], [ʁizol]
roe deer	оху	[ohu]
fallow deer	оху	[ohu]
chamois	нахчир, бузи кӯҳй	[naχtʃir], [buzi kœhi:]
wild boar	хуки ваҳши	[χuki vahʃi]

whale	кит, наҳанг	[kit], [nahang]
seal	тюлен	[tjulen]
walrus	морж	[morʒ]
fur seal	гурбаи обй	[gurbai obi:]
dolphin	делфин	[delfin]

bear	хирс	[χirs]
polar bear	хирси сафед	[χirsi safed]
panda	панда	[panda]

monkey	маймун	[majmun]
chimpanzee	шимпанзе	[ʃimpanze]
orangutan	орангутанг	[orangutang]
gorilla	горилла	[gorilla]
macaque	макака	[makaka]
gibbon	гиббон	[gibbon]

elephant	фил	[fil]
rhinoceros	карк, каркадан	[kark], [karkadan]
giraffe	заррофа	[zarrofa]
hippopotamus	баҳмут	[bahmut]

kangaroo	кенгуру	[kenguru]
koala (bear)	коала	[koala]

mongoose	росу	[rosu]
chinchilla	вашақ	[vaʃaq]
skunk	скунс	[skuns]
porcupine	чайра, дугпушт	[dʒajra], [dugpuʃt]

89. Domestic animals

cat	гурба	[gurba]
tomcat	гурбаи нар	[gurbai nar]
dog	саг	[sag]
horse	асп	[asp]
stallion (male horse)	айғир, аспи нар	[ajʁir], [aspi nar]
mare	модиён, байтал	[modijɔn], [bajtal]
cow	гов	[gov]
bull	барзагов	[barzagov]
ox	барзагов	[barzagov]
sheep (ewe)	меш, гӯсфанд	[meʃ], [gœsfand]
ram	гӯсфанд	[gœsfand]
goat	буз	[buz]
billy goat, he-goat	така, серка	[taka], [serka]
donkey	хар, маркаб	[χar], [markab]
mule	хачир	[χatʃir]
pig, hog	хук	[χuq]
piglet	хукбача	[χukbatʃa]
rabbit	харгӯш	[χargœʃ]
hen (chicken)	мурғ	[murʁ]
rooster	хурӯс	[χurœs]
duck	мурғобӣ	[murʁobi:]
drake	мурғобии нар	[murʁobi:i nar]
goose	қоз, ғоз	[qoz], [ʁoz]
tom turkey, gobbler	хурӯси мурғи марчон	[χurœsi murʁi mardʒon]
turkey (hen)	мокиёни мурғи марчон	[mokijɔni murʁi mardʒon]
domestic animals	ҳайвони хонагӣ	[hajvoni χonagi:]
tame (e.g., ~ hamster)	ромшуда	[romʃuda]
to tame (vt)	дастомӯз кардан	[dastomœz kardan]
to breed (vt)	калон кардан	[kalon kardan]
farm	ферма	[ferma]
poultry	паррандаи хонагӣ	[parrandai χonagi:]
cattle	чорво	[tʃorvo]
herd (cattle)	пода	[poda]
stable	саисхона, аспхона	[saisχona], [aspχona]
pigpen	хукхона	[χukχona]
cowshed	оғил, говхона	[oʁil], [govχona]
rabbit hutch	харгӯшхона	[χargœʃχona]
hen house	мурғхона	[murʁχona]

90. Birds

bird	паранда	[paranda]
pigeon	кафтар	[kaftar]
sparrow	гунчишк, чумчук	[gundʒiʃk], [tʃumtʃuk]
tit (great tit)	фотимачумчуқ	[fotimatʃumtʃuq]
magpie	акка	[akka]
raven	зоғ	[zoʁ]
crow	зоғи ало	[zoʁi alo]
jackdaw	зоғча	[zoʁtʃa]
rook	шӯрнӯл	[ʃœrnœl]
duck	мурғобӣ	[murʁobi:]
goose	қоз, ғоз	[qoz], [ʁoz]
pheasant	тазарв	[tazarv]
eagle	укоб	[ukob]
hawk	пайғу	[pajʁu]
falcon	боз, шоҳин	[boz], [ʃohin]
vulture	каргас	[kargas]
condor (Andean ~)	кондор	[kondor]
swan	қу	[qu]
crane	куланг, турна	[kulang], [turna]
stork	лаклак	[laklak]
parrot	тӯтӣ	[tœti:]
hummingbird	колибри	[kolibri]
peacock	товус	[tovus]
ostrich	шутурмурғ	[ʃuturmurʁ]
heron	ҳавосил	[havosil]
flamingo	бутимор	[butimor]
pelican	мурғи сакко	[murʁi saqqo]
nightingale	булбул	[bulbul]
swallow	фароштурук	[faroʃturuk]
thrush	дуррроч	[durrodʒ]
song thrush	дуррочи хушхон	[durrodʒi χuʃχon]
blackbird	дуррочи сиёҳ	[durrodʒi sijoh]
swift	досак	[dosak]
lark	чӯр, чаковак	[dʒœr], [tʃakovak]
quail	бедона	[bedona]
cuckoo	фохтак	[foχtak]
owl	бум, чуғз	[bum], [dʒuʁz]
eagle owl	чуғз	[tʃuʁz]
wood grouse	дуррроч	[durrodʒ]

| black grouse | титав | [titav] |
| partridge | кабк, каклик | [kabk], [kaklik] |

starling	сор, соч	[sor], [sotʃ]
canary	канарейка	[kanarejka]
hazel grouse	рябчик	[rjabtʃik]
chaffinch	саъва	[sa'va]
bullfinch	севғар	[sevʁar]

seagull	моҳихӯрак	[mohiχœrak]
albatross	уқоби баҳрӣ	[uqobi bahri:]
penguin	пингвин	[pingvin]

91. Fish. Marine animals

bream	симмоҳӣ	[simmohi:]
carp	капур	[kapur]
perch	аломоҳӣ	[alomohi:]
catfish	лаққамоҳӣ	[laqqamohi:]
pike	шӯртан	[ʃœrtan]

| salmon | озодмоҳӣ | [ozodmohi:] |
| sturgeon | тосмоҳӣ | [tosmohi:] |

herring	шӯрмоҳӣ	[ʃœrmohi:]
Atlantic salmon	озодмоҳӣ	[ozodmoχi:]
mackerel	зағӯтамоҳӣ	[zaʁœtamohi:]
flatfish	камбала	[kambala]

zander, pike perch	суфмоҳӣ	[sufmohi:]
cod	равғанмоҳӣ	[ravʁanmohi:]
tuna	самак	[samak]
trout	гулмоҳӣ	[gulmohi:]

eel	мормоҳӣ	[mormohi:]
electric ray	скати барқдор	[skati barqdor]
moray eel	мурена	[murena]
piranha	пираня	[piranja]

shark	наҳанг	[nahang]
dolphin	делфин	[delfin]
whale	кит, наҳанг	[kit], [nahang]

crab	харчанг	[χartʃang]
jellyfish	медуза	[meduza]
octopus	ҳаштпо	[haʃtpo]

starfish	ситораи баҳрӣ	[sitorai bahri:]
sea urchin	хорпушти баҳрӣ	[χorpuʃti bahri:]
seahorse	аспакмоҳӣ	[aspakmohi:]

oyster	садафак	[sadafak]
shrimp	креветка	[krevetka]
lobster	харчанги баҳрӣ	[ҳartʃangi bahri:]
spiny lobster	лангуст	[langust]

92. Amphibians. Reptiles

| snake | мор | [mor] |
| venomous (snake) | заҳрдор | [zahrdor] |

viper	мори афъӣ	[mori afʼi:]
cobra	мори айнакдор, кӯбро	[mori ajnakdor], [kœbro]
python	мори печон	[mori petʃon]
boa	мори печон	[mori petʃon]

grass snake	мори обӣ	[mori obi:]
rattle snake	шақшақамор	[ʃaqʃaqamor]
anaconda	анаконда	[anakonda]

lizard	калтакалос	[kaltakalos]
iguana	сусмор, игуана	[susmor], [iguana]
monitor lizard	сусмор	[susmor]
salamander	калтакалос	[kaltakalos]
chameleon	бӯқаламун	[bœqalamun]
scorpion	каждум	[kaʒdum]

turtle	сангпушт	[sangpuʃt]
frog	қурбоққа	[qurboqqa]
toad	ғук, қурбоққаи чӯлӣ	[ʁuk], [qurboqqai tʃœli:]
crocodile	тимсоҳ	[timsoh]

93. Insects

insect, bug	ҳашарот	[haʃarot]
butterfly	шапалак	[ʃapalak]
ant	мӯрча	[mœrtʃa]
fly	магас	[magas]
mosquito	пашша	[paʃʃa]
beetle	гамбуск	[gambusk]

wasp	ору	[oru]
bee	занбӯри асал	[zanbœri asal]
bumblebee	говзанбӯр	[govzanbœr]
gadfly (botfly)	ғурмагас	[ʁurmagas]

spider	тортанак	[tortanak]
spiderweb	тори тортанак	[tori tortanak]
dragonfly	сӯзанак	[sœzanak]

| grasshopper | малах | [malaχ] |
| moth (night butterfly) | шапалак | [ʃapalak] |

cockroach	нонхӯрак	[nonχœrak]
tick	кана	[kana]
flea	кайк	[kajk]
midge	пашша	[paʃʃa]

locust	малах	[malaχ]
snail	тӯкумшуллуқ	[tœkumʃulluq]
cricket	чирчирак	[tʃirtʃirak]
lightning bug	шабтоб	[ʃabtob]
ladybug	момохолак	[momoχolak]
cockchafer	гамбуски саврӣ	[gambuski savri:]

leech	шуллук	[ʃulluk]
caterpillar	кирм	[kirm]
earthworm	кирм	[kirm]
larva	кирм	[kirm]

FLORA

94. Trees

tree	дарахт	[daraχt]
deciduous (adj)	паҳнбарг	[pahnbarg]
coniferous (adj)	… и сӯзанбарг	[i sœzanbarg]
evergreen (adj)	ҳамешасабз	[hameʃasabz]
apple tree	дарахти себ	[daraχti seb]
pear tree	дарахти нок	[daraχti nok]
sweet cherry tree	дарахти гелос	[daraχti gelos]
sour cherry tree	дарахти олубулу	[daraχti olubulu]
plum tree	дарахти олу	[daraχti olu]
birch	тӯс	[tœs]
oak	булут	[bulut]
linden tree	зерфун	[zerfun]
aspen	сиёхбед	[sijohbed]
maple	заранг	[zarang]
spruce	коч, ел	[koʤ], [el]
pine	санавбар	[sanavbar]
larch	кочи баргрез	[koʤi bargrez]
fir tree	пихта	[piχta]
cedar	дарахти чалгӯза	[daraχti ʤalʁœza]
poplar	сафедор	[safedor]
rowan	губайро	[ʁubajro]
willow	бед	[bed]
alder	роздор	[rozdor]
beech	бук, олаш	[buk], [olaʃ]
elm	дарахти ларг	[daraχti larg]
ash (tree)	шумтол	[ʃumtol]
chestnut	шохбулут	[ʃohbulut]
magnolia	магнолия	[magnolija]
palm tree	нахл	[naχl]
cypress	дарахти сарв	[daraχti sarv]
mangrove	дарахти анбаҳ	[daraχti anbah]
baobab	баобаб	[baobab]
eucalyptus	эвкалипт	[ɛvkalipt]
sequoia	секвойя	[sekvojja]

95. Shrubs

bush	бутта	[butta]
shrub	бутта	[butta]
grapevine	ток	[tok]
vineyard	токзор	[tokzor]
raspberry bush	тамашк	[tamaʃk]
blackcurrant bush	қоти сиёҳ	[qoti sijɔh]
redcurrant bush	коти сурх	[koti surχ]
gooseberry bush	бектошӣ	[bektoʃi:]
acacia	акатсия, акоқиё	[akatsija], [aqoqijɔ]
barberry	буттаи зирк	[buttai zirk]
jasmine	ёсуман	[jɔsuman]
juniper	арча, ардач	[arʧa], [ardaʤ]
rosebush	буттаи гул	[buttai gul]
dog rose	хуч	[χutʃ]

96. Fruits. Berries

fruit	мева, самар	[meva], [samar]
fruits	меваҳо, самарҳо	[mevaho], [samarho]
apple	себ	[seb]
pear	мурӯд, нок	[murœd], [nok]
plum	олу	[olu]
strawberry (garden ~)	қулфинай	[qulfinaj]
sour cherry	олуболу	[olubolu]
sweet cherry	гелос	[gelos]
grape	ангур	[angur]
raspberry	тамашк	[tamaʃk]
blackcurrant	қоти сиёҳ	[qoti sijɔh]
redcurrant	коти сурх	[koti surχ]
gooseberry	бектошӣ	[bektoʃi:]
cranberry	клюква	[kljukva]
orange	афлесун, пӯртахол	[aflesun], [pœrtaχol]
mandarin	норанг	[norang]
pineapple	ананас	[ananas]
banana	банан	[banan]
date	хурмо	[χurmo]
lemon	лиму	[limu]
apricot	дарахти зардолу	[daraχti zardolu]

peach	шафтолу	[ʃaftolu]
kiwi	кивй	[kivi:]
grapefruit	норинҷ	[norindʒ]

berry	буттамева	[buttameva]
berries	буттамеваҳо	[buttamevaho]
cowberry	брусника	[brusnika]
wild strawberry	тути заминй	[tuti zamini:]
bilberry	черника	[tʃernika]

97. Flowers. Plants

| flower | гул | [gul] |
| bouquet (of flowers) | дастаи гул | [dastai gul] |

rose (flower)	гул, гули садбарг	[gul], [guli sadbarg]
tulip	лола	[lola]
carnation	гули меҳак	[guli meχak]
gladiolus	гули ёқут	[guli jɔqut]

cornflower	тугмагул	[tugmagul]
harebell	гули момо	[guli momo]
dandelion	коқу	[koqu]
camomile	бобуна	[bobuna]

aloe	уд, сабр, алоэ	[ud], [sabr], [alɔɛ]
cactus	гули ханҷарй	[guli χandʒari:]
rubber plant, ficus	тутанҷир	[tutandʒir]

lily	савсан	[savsan]
geranium	анҷибар	[andʒibar]
hyacinth	сунбул	[sunbul]

mimosa	нозгул	[nozgul]
narcissus	наргис	[nargis]
nasturtium	настаран	[nastaran]

orchid	саҳлаб, сӯҳлаб	[sahlab], [sœhlab]
peony	гули ашрафй	[guli aʃrafi:]
violet	бунафша	[bunafʃa]

pansy	бунафшаи фарангй	[bunafʃai farangi:]
forget-me-not	марзангӯш	[marzangœʃ]
daisy	гули марворидак	[guli marvoridak]

poppy	кӯкнор	[kœknor]
hemp	бангдона, канаб	[bangdona], [kanab]
mint	пудина	[pudina]
lily of the valley	гули барфак	[guli barfak]
snowdrop	бойчечак	[bojtʃetʃak]

nettle	газна	[gazna]
sorrel	шилха	[ʃilχa]
water lily	нилуфари сафед	[nilufari safed]
fern	фарн	[farn]
lichen	гулсанг	[gulsang]

greenhouse (tropical ~)	гулхона	[gulχona]
lawn	чаман, сабзазор	[tʃaman], [sabzazor]
flowerbed	гулзор	[gulzor]

plant	растанй	[rastani:]
grass	алаф	[alaf]
blade of grass	хас	[χas]

leaf	барг	[barg]
petal	гулбарг	[gulbarg]
stem	поя	[poja]
tuber	бех, дона	[beχ], [dona]

| young plant (shoot) | неш | [neʃ] |
| thorn | хор | [χor] |

to blossom (vi)	гул кардан	[gul kardan]
to fade, to wither	пажмурда шудан	[paʒmurda ʃudan]
smell (odor)	бӯй	[bœj]
to cut (flowers)	буридан	[buridan]
to pick (a flower)	кандан	[kandan]

98. Cereals, grains

grain	дона, ғалла	[dona], [ʁalla]
cereal crops	растаниҳои ғалладона	[rastanihoi ʁalladona]
ear (of barley, etc.)	хӯша	[χœʃa]

wheat	гандум	[gandum]
rye	чавдор	[dʒavdor]
oats	хуртумон	[hurtumon]

| millet | арзан | [arzan] |
| barley | чав | [dʒav] |

corn	чуворимакка	[dʒuvorimakka]
rice	шолй, биринч	[ʃoli:], [birindʒ]
buckwheat	марчумак	[mardʒumak]

pea plant	нахӯд	[naχœd]
kidney bean	лӯбиё	[lœbijo]
soy	соя	[soja]
lentil	наск	[nask]
beans (pulse crops)	лӯбиё	[lœbijo]

COUNTRIES OF THE WORLD

99. Countries. Part 1

Afghanistan	Афғонистон	[afʁoniston]
Albania	Албания	[albanija]
Argentina	Аргентина	[argentina]
Armenia	Арманистон	[armaniston]
Australia	Австралия	[avstralija]
Austria	Австрия	[avstrija]
Azerbaijan	Озарбойҷон	[ozarbojdʒon]
The Bahamas	Ҷазираҳои Багам	[dʒazirahoi bagam]
Bangladesh	Бангладеш	[bangladeʃ]
Belarus	Беларус	[belarus]
Belgium	Белгия	[belgija]
Bolivia	Боливия	[bolivija]
Bosnia and Herzegovina	Босния ва Херсеговина	[bosnija va hersegovina]
Brazil	Бразилия	[brazilija]
Bulgaria	Булғористон	[bulʁoriston]
Cambodia	Камбоҷа	[kambodʒa]
Canada	Канада	[kanada]
Chile	Чиле	[tʃile]
China	Чин	[tʃin]
Colombia	Колумбия	[kolumbija]
Croatia	Хорватия	[χorvatija]
Cuba	Куба	[kuba]
Cyprus	Кипр	[kipr]
Czech Republic	Чехия	[tʃeχija]
Denmark	Дания	[danija]
Dominican Republic	Ҷумхурии Доминикан	[dʒumhuri:i dominikan]
Ecuador	Эквадор	[ɛkvador]
Egypt	Миср	[misr]
England	Англия	[anglija]
Estonia	Эстония	[ɛstonija]
Finland	Финланд	[finland]
France	Фаронса	[faronsa]
French Polynesia	Полинезияи Фаронсавӣ	[polinezijai faronsavi:]
Georgia	Гурҷистон	[gurdʒiston]
Germany	Олмон	[olmon]
Ghana	Гана	[gana]
Great Britain	Инглистон	[ingliston]

Greece	Юнон	[junon]
Haiti	Гаити	[gaiti]
Hungary	Маҷористон	[madʒoriston]

100. Countries. Part 2

Iceland	Исландия	[islandija]
India	Ҳиндустон	[hinduston]
Indonesia	Индонезия	[indonezija]
Iran	Эрон	[ɛron]
Iraq	Ироқ	[iroq]
Ireland	Ирландия	[irlandija]
Israel	Исроил	[isroil]
Italy	Итолиё	[itolijɔ]

Jamaica	Ямайка	[jamajka]
Japan	Жопун, Чопон	[ʒopun], [dʒopon]
Jordan	Урдун	[urdun]
Kazakhstan	Қазоқистон	[qazoqiston]
Kenya	Кения	[kenija]
Kirghizia	Қирғизистон	[qirʁiziston]
Kuwait	Кувайт	[kuvajt]

Laos	Лаос	[laos]
Latvia	Латвия	[latvija]
Lebanon	Лубнон	[lubnon]
Libya	Либия	[libija]
Liechtenstein	Лихтенштейн	[liхtenʃtejn]
Lithuania	Литва	[litva]
Luxembourg	Люксембург	[ljuksemburg]

Macedonia (Republic of ~)	Мақдуния	[maqdunija]
Madagascar	Мадагаскар	[madagaskar]
Malaysia	Малайзия	[malajzija]
Malta	Малта	[malta]
Mexico	Мексика	[meksika]
Moldova, Moldavia	Молдова	[moldova]

Monaco	Монако	[monako]
Mongolia	Муғулистон	[muʁuliston]
Montenegro	Монтенегро	[montenegro]
Morocco	Марокаш	[marokaʃ]
Myanmar	Мянма	[mjanma]

Namibia	Намибия	[namibija]
Nepal	Непал	[nepal]
Netherlands	Ҳоланд	[holand]
New Zealand	Зеландияи Нав	[zelandijai nav]
North Korea	Кореяи Шимолӣ	[korejai ʃimoli:]
Norway	Норвегия	[norvegija]

101. Countries. Part 3

Pakistan	Покистон	[pokiston]
Palestine	Фаластин	[falastin]
Panama	Панама	[panama]
Paraguay	Парагвай	[paragvaj]
Peru	Перу	[peru]
Poland	Полша, Лаҳистон	[polʃa], [lahiston]
Portugal	Португалия	[portugalija]
Romania	Руминия	[ruminija]
Russia	Россия	[rossija]

Saudi Arabia	Арабистони Саудӣ	[arabistoni saudi:]
Scotland	Шотландия	[ʃotlandija]
Senegal	Сенегал	[senegal]
Serbia	Сербия	[serbija]
Slovakia	Словакия	[slovakija]
Slovenia	Словения	[slovenija]

South Africa	Африқои Ҷанубӣ	[afriqoi dʒanubi:]
South Korea	Кореяи Ҷанубӣ	[korejai dʒanubi:]
Spain	Испониё	[isponijɔ]
Suriname	Суринам	[surinam]
Sweden	Шветсия	[ʃvetsija]
Switzerland	Швейсария	[ʃvejsarija]
Syria	Сурия	[surija]

Taiwan	Тайван	[tajvan]
Tajikistan	Тоҷикистон	[todʒikiston]
Tanzania	Танзания	[tanzanija]
Tasmania	Тасмания	[tasmanija]
Thailand	Таиланд	[tailand]
Tunisia	Тунис	[tunis]
Turkey	Туркия	[turkija]
Turkmenistan	Туркманистон	[turkmaniston]

Ukraine	Украйина	[ukrajina]
United Arab Emirates	Иморатҳои Муттаҳидаи Араб	[imorathoi muttahidai arab]
United States of America	Иёлоти Муттаҳидаи Америка	[ijɔloti muttahidai amerika]
Uruguay	Уругвай	[urugvaj]
Uzbekistan	Ӯзбакистон	[œzbakiston]

Vatican	Вотикон	[votikon]
Venezuela	Венесуэла	[venesuɛla]
Vietnam	Ветнам	[vetnam]
Zanzibar	Занзибар	[zanzibar]

Made in United States
North Haven, CT
16 July 2023

39155469R00063